BOOK SOLD
NO LONGER R H P.L.
PROPERTY

By Elissa Altman

Motherland

Treyf

Poor Man's Feast

Motherland

Motherland

A Memoir of
Love, Loathing,
and Longing

...

Elissa Altman

BALLANTINE BOOKS | NEW YORK

This is a work of memoir, which is an act of memory rather than history. The events and experiences rendered here are all true as the author has recalled them to the best of her ability, and as older stories were related to her over the years. Some names, identifying characteristics, and circumstances have been changed in order to protect the privacy of individuals involved.

Copyright © 2019 by Elissa Altman

All rights reserved.

Published in the United States by Ballantine Books, an imprint of Random House, a division of Penguin Random House LLC, New York.

BALLANTINE and the HOUSE colophon are registered trademarks of Penguin Random House LLC.

The Girl is used by grateful permission from the author, Marie Howe.

LIBRARY OF CONGRESS CATALOGING-IN-PUBLICATION DATA
Names: Altman, Elissa, author.
Title: Motherland : a memoir of love, loathing, and longing / Elissa Altman.
Description: First edition. | New York : Ballantine Books, [2019]
Identifiers: LCCN 2019007425 |
ISBN 9780399181580 (hardcover : alk. paper) | ISBN 9780399181597 (ebook)
Subjects: LCSH: Altman, Elissa. | Altman, Elissa—Family. | Women caregivers—United States—Biography. | Mothers and daughters—United States—Biography. | Codependency. | Women authors, American—Biography. | Lesbians—United States—Biography. | New York (N.Y.)—Biography. | Connecticut—Biography.
Classification: LCC CT275.A624 A3 2019 | DDC 306.874/3092 [B]—dc23
LC record available at https://lccn.loc.gov/2019007425

Printed in the United States of America on acid-free paper

randomhousebooks.com

2 4 6 8 9 7 5 3 1

First Edition

Book design by Susan Turner

RICHMOND HILL PUBLIC LIBRARY
3297 2001484601   RH
Motherland : a memoir of love, loathing,
Jul. 30, 2019

For my mother, now and always

So close to the end of my childbearing life
without children

—if I could remember a day when I was utterly a girl
and not yet a woman—

but I don't think there was a day like that for me.

When I look at the girl I was, dripping in her bathing suit,
or riding her bike, pumping hard down the newly paved street,

she wears a furtive look—
and even if I could go back in time to her as me, the age I am now

she would never come into my arms
without believing that I wanted something.

—MARIE HOWE, *The Girl*

Mother

(1) a: a female parent

    b: a woman in higher authority; specifically:
the superior of a religious community of women

(2) an older or elderly woman

(3) source, origin

(4) maternal tenderness or affection

(5) vulgar

(6) something that is an extreme or ultimate example
of its kind specifically in terms of scale
<the mother of all projects>

(7) vinegar or sourdough starter

Also:

Mother sauce

Mother tongue

Motherboard

Mother ship

Mother lode

Mother love

Motherfucker

Preface

I WAS BORN WITH A SMALL IRREGULAR SPOT ON MY FIFTH RIB, beneath my left breast and below the ventricular, arrhythmic tip of my heart. The color of a faint lavender bruise, it is shaped like a triangle; a nick in a piece of old furniture.

"You were supposed to be a twin," my father said. "That's probably all that's left of her."

He told me this over a pastrami sandwich at our local delicatessen in Forest Hills, New York, where we lived in a brick apartment building the color of a pencil eraser; it was the early seventies, and I was a young child, still in single digits. The air between us was humid with sauerkraut and Cel-Ray fumes, and I placed my hand over the mark and closed my eyes. I imagined who she might have been and what she might have looked like. I swore to protect her in a way I can only now describe as maternal.

As a child, I wore this mark like a badge of unfulfilled promise. I believed that she, this disfigurement, was the one I was supposed to be, the one who could have made my mother happy and eased her yearning.

Motherland

I

Love doesn't just sit there, like a stone, it has to be made, like bread; remade all the time, made new.

—URSULA K. LE GUIN, *The Lathe of Heaven*

1

MY CONNECTICUT KITCHEN IN THE EARLY MORNING.

My wife and I live where it is quiet, not quite rural, not
quite suburban, where a car driving down the street in the
middle of the day is cause for wonder and, because I am
still a New Yorker at heart, for the locking of the front door.
Recently, we bought a heavy-duty deadbolt—we'd never had
one—because the previous owner, who built our little house
on an acre in 1971, had installed a simple push-button bedroom lock on the hollow-core front door. It wasn't that he
was cheap; there was just no reason to have anything more
secure. He didn't want to court karmic trouble by kitting out
his home like Fort Knox. He was safe here, he told us, with
his wife and two growing daughters.

When Susan and I came to look at the house on a snowy February afternoon in 2004, the owner, in his late eighties and wearing a black-and-red wool hunting coat and a green camouflage knit cap, leaned his wooden cane against one of the front pillars, pulled a massive gas-powered snow blower out of the garage and carved a wide path for us to safely walk side by side around the property. He apologized for the state of his beloved rhododendrons and azaleas, which had recently been devoured by deer but were nonetheless neatly wrapped up like cigars from top to bottom in garden burlap as if to protect the possibility that they might flower again when the season changed; gardening is a contract with hope.

The man's wife, a laconic blue-eyed woman just beginning to forget, gave us a swatch of the original yellow-and-silver-striped wallpaper, in case we ever needed to match it. They had led a good life here, the man said, and were downsizing to a nearby retirement community; one daughter was moving to England and the other to a small village in the Berkshire foothills. They were proud of their home, but soft-spoken and humble in the way Yankees tend to be.

Except for removing the wallpaper, we touched nothing else for years, including the girls' bedrooms, whose walls still bore the vinyl-flowered adhesive evidence of their childhood. We eventually turned one room into my office and the other into a book-lined guestroom that I envisioned someday containing a simple Shaker-style crib, a rocking chair, a changing table. We even took chances with the lock until I began to work from home. Susan and I had thrown caution to the wind because security and safety can be such a myth; trouble can come from anywhere.

———

In the years that Susan and I have been in this house, I have learned the seasonal trajectory of light, which in the morning streams through the dining room window onto our ancient barnwood table in one harsh bolt. By sundown, it glares through the living room in an explosion so bright that it's often hard to see the house across the street. Our life here is slow and quiet, and, for two women together nineteen years, conventional. My work is solitary; when I'm writing, I can sit at my desk and not get up for hours, until the sun has made its circle around the house. A clock isn't necessary. I know what time it is by the cast of light on the walls.

On this day, the sun isn't all the way up, and the interior of the house is a murky gray. I have just come in from a run. I was never a runner, but I began recently because it creates a kind of porosity; it allows air and light to filter through me and loosens the knot that snares me every morning before eight when I answer the phone, in the slim moment between the ring and the sound of my mother's voice. A rest; a beat. A break in the symbiosis that has defined us and the universe in which we've lived. I stand in my kitchen and stare at the phone. I inhale. It rings. The dog barks. I exhale. I choose my response—*the seconds between stimulus and reaction,* Viktor Frankl called it—in which lies my freedom.

Like the Centralia Mine fire, my mother and I have been burning for half a century.

We draw life from the heart of battle, a dopamine helix that propels us forward, breathing air into our days like a bel-

lows. Some Buddhists say that anger is good when it is genera-
tive; if so, the warring to which we are addicted has enlivened
us and built up our muscle memory, like the hands of a boxer.
We bob and weave; we love and we loathe; we shout and whisper, and the next morning we do it all over again. Like tying our
shoes or brushing our teeth or shaving one leg before the other,
this is our ritual, our habit. We know no other way.

"What is your intoxicant of choice?" I was once asked at an
AA meeting. I sat on a rusting beige metal folding chair in the
basement of a white clapboard Congregational church in rural
Connecticut, drinking cold coffee out of a Styrofoam cup.
"Wine? Scotch? Beer before breakfast? Shopping? Porn?"

"My mother," I whispered.

People shifted; they held their chins.

My mother.

Lead a simple life, a neurologist advises Joan Didion in *The
White Album,* when she begins in middle age to suffer from a
nervous disorder with symptoms she describes as being *usually
associated with telethons. Not that it makes any difference we
know about,* the doctor adds. *Leading a simple life* may be nothing more than placebo, a psychogenic bandage under which
one is able to catch one's breath and find one's footing. I'd
moved to the country because I'd fallen in love with someone
who lived there, but also to find the peace that I had so longed
for; I fled my hometown of ten million for a village of three
thousand. I was settled, but also easily startled, like a battle
veteran returning to the suburbs from the front. Instead of
spending my days traversing Manhattan in stony silence, my
mother's delicate arm hooked in mine as we gazed into the

shop windows along Madison Avenue, I worked in my win-
dowed basement office that looked out onto Susan's shed, blan-
keted with the white Pierre de Ronsard climbing roses we'd
planted the summer before I left the city. We spent days together, side by side in our overgrown garden; I pulled weeds in
dazed shock. My sleep began to grow fitful and my hands trem-
bled when I drank my morning coffee. Where my mother had
regularly called me four or five times every day and often waited
for me to get home from work in my apartment building lobby,
we now spoke only morning and night and saw each other
every other week. Bitter recriminations flew. *How could I have
left? When was I coming back? How dare I go.* While Susan
slept soundly next to me in our bed two hours away from everything I'd once known, I was jolted awake at 3:23 every morning, sweaty and disoriented, my heart pounding hard as though
I'd been grabbed by the shoulders and shaken from a night
terror. I would scuttle down the stairs to the kitchen and pour
myself a small juice glass of red wine, which I'd drink while
sitting on the couch in the dark next to the dog.

Wine had become a third party, a witness, a fly on my wall.
The fiercer the battles with my mother, the deeper my thirst;
the more wine I had, the more firmly I held my ground. My
father, divorced from my mother after sixteen years of marriage, had introduced me to French Burgundies during our
custodial weekends alone together. At fifteen, I furtively sipped
his glasses of Gevrey-Chambertin between bites of cassoulet at
fancy Manhattan restaurants, and the world was serene. With
my mother, I drank either to sleep or to get drunk, to dull the
blade, and the world got angry. Awakened in the middle of

every night, I became an insomniac; I needed a fix. I poured myself a small glass, sat on the couch, and called her to make sure that we were okay.

It was not the alcohol to which I was addicted; it was she, and together we fed on our affection and rage like buttered popcorn. I suckled on my mother's beautiful fury; it fed me and nourished me. We clung to the silent compact that neither of us would ever abandon the other, no matter what.

Until I did.

I had the audacity to leave New York City for good, to find love and happiness elsewhere. To make a home and family at which she was not at the center. To leave her for another woman.

It had been a choice: my mother's life, or my own.

. . .

IN MY HOME, WE WERE three: mother, father, daughter. There were books; my father's gold-spined Reader's Digest Condensed Editions lined every shelf, sandwiched between Philip Roth and Henry Miller. Every month from the time I was four, a *My Weekly Reader* paperback selection arrived in the mail with my name on it. We listened to Trini Lopez and Peggy Lee, the Modern Jazz Quartet and Judy Garland, on my father's teak Garrard turntable, and my mother sang along. We had annual memberships to a local pool club, MoMA, and the Smithsonian. Piles of *Vogue, Life, Harper's Bazaar, Modern Photography,* and *The New Yorker* were stacked in every corner of the living room and on the floor in front of the toilets in both bathrooms. My short, corpulent father, possessed of a violent temper that could turn with the direction of the wind, was witty and cerebral, deeply affectionate and clinically depressed, in love with *Commentary* and Irving Kristol and the perceived safety of intellectual Jewish conservative tradition. He ran twice for local office as an Independent, stumping for unpopular causes, and failed.

My mother had been, for thirteen weeks in 1957, a national television star; she was the fair-haired all-American girl singer on a Saturday night variety show, the precursor to Andy Williams and Carol Burnett, and her job was to step out on the live sound stage and do as her boss, Galen Drake, asked: *Sing us a song about this terrible rainy weather, Rita,* he'd say, and she would. Her appearance on television defined her and was the focal point of our family dinnertime conversation. As a child, I longed to see her on the other side of the screen, where everyone seemed perfect and happy; I spent every Saturday night turning the television dial, looking for her show even though it had been canceled five years before I was born. She was a myth I searched for and never found.

My mother was elegant, preternaturally thin, pouty, and so radiant—unlike my friends' mothers: older, round, dour women with the trauma of war still lingering in their eyes—that one had to squint to see her clearly, as though her vibrancy made it too dangerous to look directly at her without corneal injury. Propelled through life on the fuel of desire and regret, she was beautiful and stylish in a way that seemed unreal, as though she had stepped out of the pages of a Diana Vreeland editorial feature. She stopped traffic; handsome men I vaguely knew flagged her down and crossed the broad, dangerous boulevard that ran east to west through our town in order to speak to her. While my father carried himself with an air of studied formality, my mother was devilishly, fabulously flirty; even young children can detect innuendo in the set of a jaw. When we walked together down the streets of our neighborhood, I was proud to be hers, to be *of* her, to be seen alongside her. I held her hand; waiting to cross the street, she lifted it affectionately to kiss mine. We strolled side by side; I watched her closely, as though I were looking at the moon and searching for evidence of life.

My mother said hello to no woman unless they acknowledged her first; only then would she respond to them and stop to talk, placing her hands on my narrow shoulders and positioning me in front of her like a shield. Conversations were warm and friendly and then, inevitably, slithered down the slope of competition; they grew quietly seething and tempestuous. An acquaintance with a new outfit, a new hairstyle, a new boyfriend, a new lipstick could send her into a tailspin for days until, relieved by an impulse unharnessed—a new coat for me that I didn't need, a set of engraved Tiffany stationery for her— she was soothed like a junkie with a hit of heroin. My mother was strategic and gamine; her illusoriness terrified and delighted me, as though she were an automaton at Disneyland whose controls could at any moment go haywire.

Photograph: 1971. My cousin Beth's wedding at the Fifth Avenue Hotel in Greenwich Village. My mother and I wear matching lace mother-daughter jumpsuits; she rests her hand lovingly on the small of my back. Tall and wraithlike, she smiles at the camera, her blond hair pulled back tightly in a George. My father, in his tuxedo, shifts toward his beautiful wife, the right side of his face obscured like the dark side of the moon, filled with astonishment and pride that this woman, his wife—*his* wife—is so stunning that every man in the room stares at her, coughs, and claps my father's shoulder like football players in a locker room. Two months after a bicycle accident that nearly killed me, I stand in front of them in the lower left corner of the photo. Although I am dressed like my mother, I resemble my father—I am the image of him, a scaled-down, female replica with long blond hair and his round face. I am eight years old, smiling maniacally, my right cheek partially shrouded in bruising, my eyes squeezed tight against the impossible joy of it all, the three of us posed together in front of a camera. A record of a single happy day, my mother's lovely face, dewy with makeup, in the spotlight: The camera loves her and finds her full-on. We, her husband and child, hide in the penumbra, partially seen and partially not.

A light here requires a shadow there, said Mrs. Ramsay.

We arrive at the party hopeful for love: dressed identically, a beautiful young mother in her early thirties and her eight-year-old daughter. We are jubilant. We dance a vigorous hora while the bride and groom are thrust high into the air on wooden chairs; our circle of family careens violently in one direction and then the other. My father's sister, the stately and formal family matriarch, older than he by five years, her hair teased into a tall auburn aureole, dances a slow Russian *sher* with her sisters-in-law. My father's father, an Orthodox cantor with one foot in the old world and one in the new, slices the celebratory challah and says the *motzi*.

"I was once a star," my mother tells the guests who mill around us in a throng, drinking whiskey sour highballs and crimson Shirley Temples and eating pigs in blankets by the fistful.

It's true, I insist, as if the fact of my mother's talent might dare be questioned by anyone in the room. I am her protector, her keeper. I swing off her arm like a much younger child; she smiles down at me and cups my chin, and a rush of warmth fills my heart.

My Lissie, she says. *My darling Lissie.*

The main course arrives. The photographer makes his rounds with a massive Polaroid medium-format camera and snaps a picture. My mother asks my father for a cigarette; she is suddenly nervous and fretful, and her hands quiver. He gives her one of his Parliaments, leans across her untouched plate— chicken breast and green beans amandine, perhaps, which are now getting cold—strikes a match, and lights it. She smokes it halfway down and stubs it out hard into a glass ashtray. She is no longer smiling. The air around her suddenly crackles like a hot wire; so much joy, and then a plunge. I shiver. If she is not asked to sing with the wedding band, to coil the microphone cord around one hand the way she once did so expertly years earlier when it was her job, the joy of the day will wither like an autumn leaf, and the mood shift from celebration to catastrophe.

My mother taps her foot beneath the table and grows antsy as a child waiting for Christmas morning; she squirms, hoping for someone to ask her to get up. I cross my fingers under the table. *Please, someone, ask her to sing,* I pray. *Please.* She couldn't possibly ask the bandleader herself—that isn't for a lady to do, and at this point in her life, after the television show and all the awards, all the things she gave up to be here in this moment, at this time, she shouldn't have to. As the meal draws to a close and we are picking at the wedding cake, a distant relative— a dentist we see only at weddings and funerals—comes along, leans over, and whispers in her ear, just as she's given up all hope that it will ever happen. She nods; she smiles. I leap from my seat and clap. My father, so proud of her, catches the eye of his sister, who glares at him from across the room. My mother stands and straightens her jumpsuit. I watch as she walks to the bandstand—it seems to take forever for her to get up there—her eyes cast downward and humble—*Who, me? Why, thank you*—while the room grows silent. My father and I sit on the edges of our chairs, in awe. She is ours; she belongs to *us.* We belong to her. Someone—a waiter? an aunt?—whispers while my mother begins the opening notes of "Life Is a Caba-ret." Her eyes scan the room for the offender; she stumbles over the words. She falters and shakes her head; a disaster. The light around us fades.

I used to have a girlfriend known as Chelsea. With whom I shared four sordid rooms in Chelsea.

Elsie, I whisper. *Ma, it's Elsie.*

She nods at me and winks, finishes the song, and strides off the bandstand. Cousins roar with applause and delight, but she doesn't hear them. She gathers me and our things—we leave the table flowers behind (she's allergic); she stuffs a blue crushed velvet yarmulke into her purse—while my father pulls the Buick around in front of the awning. I kiss my cousins and my grandparents goodbye. My mother tells them she is feeling unwell. We leave quietly and drive home in silence. When we arrive, she removes her makeup with thick white dollops of Noxzema, weeping over her bathroom sink at the futility of it all. *Why does she even bother.* She closes the bathroom door. The lock clicks.

"I will *never* sing again," she cries. "I will *never* be a performer."

"But you're so *good,* Mom," I say, sitting on her bed while my father is out walking the dog. "Everyone *loved* you—"

Never again, she cries. *Never. My life is over.*

My first small death. She will never recover from this; her life is over, she said. The ache in my stomach—as though my core is being peeled apart, layer by layer, like an old onion—is the distillation of grief. I want to save her, to reassemble her soul like the pieces of a shattered vase. I want to make her whole the way she once was before all this, when she was in front of the camera, in the publicity clippings that sit in an album in the hallway closet, from long before I was born. I want to return her to herself.

My mother is beauty and she is music, and I love her to my bones. If she is broken, we are both broken. If she is whole, we are whole.

· · ·

I GREW UP IN THE way immigrant children do, caught between the lexicon of two worlds, the language of the past and the present. I metabolized the foreign syntax of resentment and unfulfilled appetites that my mother spoke in every sentence; I secretly yearned for the mundane and the serene, the tedious B side to an extraordinary universe whose angry dialect fell from my young lips like a dying native tongue.

To be the child of such splendor and love and rage—to be kin to it, its daughter—is to live in a world of magical thinking, with the belief that one has the power to right the ship and straighten its course. It would take me a lifetime to understand that my mother was at the helm of her own craft, and that she alone could sail it into the wind or run it aground.

And so, in these quiet years of my midlife in Connecticut, two hours from my mother, I have started to run, and its markers—time and distance—have become my healers, my lodestars. The passage of time repairs the heart; distance sharpens the lens of clarity. A serious athlete in my younger years, I habitually pushed my body to the point of collapse in order to free it from the constraints of psychic ownership and claim, to remind it that it belonged to nothing and no one but its actual owner. One afternoon in Connecticut while writing my second book, I stood up from my desk, laced on a pair of old running shoes I found in the hallway closet, and ran around our cul-de-sac. I panted and perspired and felt as though my heart was going to explode out of my chest. A week later, a half mile became whole, and one mile became two. My lungs filled with life, and pain became pleasure. I run to flee our story, to groove a new habit.

On this autumn morning in 2017, a year after my mother's accident that will cause a seismic shift in our lives, I kick off my sneakers in the entryway of my home and walk into the kitchen and make myself a cup of coffee. An ordinary workday in late fall. Petey, our rescued terrier mutt, waits at my feet for his breakfast; he stares up at me intensely, unblinking. Susan is on the train, on her way to her job in Manhattan. Outside, the vegetable garden is beginning to die. My days here are contented and quiet.

After the accident, I became consumed by my mother's physical needs where I had once only been consumed by the ferocity of her love. Two surgeries and months of rehabilitation and I was sucked back in by a force that had taken me decades to escape. *A moral obligation,* I called it. *The right thing to do. She gave you life,* my friends said. My mother's only child, now in my fifties—we are all that remains of our small New York family—I fought for this life with Susan and our home in the hills of New England. Some would say I ran.

While the coffee drips into my Chemex, I sift through a thick rubber-banded stack of my mother's bills and statements, letters and notices: the reduction of a kaleidoscopic world of need and promise to the purely practical—facts, figures, numbers—of which I am in charge. I am now her keeper. I say yes, and I say no.

My left hand holds my right, to steady it. The phone rings.

2

"THIS IS NOT HOW MOTHERS AND DAUGHTERS BEHAVE," MY
father says.

He is sitting at our breakfast counter, reading the paper,
drinking Sanka out of an orange melamine cup, eating a soft-
boiled egg into which he is dunking a narrow slice of crumbling
diet white bread.

It is early in the morning, a school day. It is in the late fall of
1974, eight months after Patty Hearst is kidnapped by the Sym-
bionese Liberation Army. The word *cult* has entered our vocabulary; there are stories everywhere of children running off,
disappearing, vanishing without a trace. My father has installed
a series of extra locks on the door; the weather is getting cold.

My mother and I are morning warriors. Neither of us
likes to leave our beds—we still don't; morning is so

unpredictable—and our sleep, in rooms across a narrow hallway separated by a bathroom, is fitful. My father is an early riser, lighthearted and optimistic—*Good morning, girls,* he bellows—a hunter-gatherer of bagels and lox who walks our Airedale while listening to the news on a tiny plastic transistor radio that he carries in his suit pocket. My mother and I wake dry-mouthed and drunk with the assumption of regret; we open our eyes and expect recrimination. We have little else in common. We are genetically disposed to surprise and suspicion when the morning is pleasant and the air sweet.

"School, honey," she says, shaking my shoulder. I lie in bed, eyes open, unblinking, staring at the ceiling.

"Get up. Honey. School."

Coffee and eggs, Hawaiian Punch, a vitamin in the shape of Wilma Flintstone. My mother has left a tiny brown Bloomingdale's shopping bag of makeup samples on my bathroom sink, where I can't miss it, on top of a box of caramel-flavored AYDS diet candies. I wash my face with a special, expensive black soap. I leave the makeup untouched. I choose an outfit for myself from the bowels of my closet, which is overstuffed with tiny fake Pucci dresses, blue suede miniskirts, rabbit fur vests, see-through voile blouses, and high leather boots from an equestrian shop in the city. I shove everything out of the way, put on a dark brown double-breasted tweed suit, and appear in the kitchen. My mother stands at the sink and scans me up and down.

"Eat your breakfast, darling," she says, turning away.

She bites her lip and shakes her head. She squeezes her eyes shut. My father eats in silence and reads the paper. I sit down next to him.

A white rubber spatula, crisp and brown around its edges from years of flipping our fried eggs, cartwheels through the air past the glass percolator and careens off the kitchen wall clock in the shape of a daisy. I jump off my breakfast stool. My father grabs his coffee cup and pushes himself away from the counter.

Dammit, Rita—

"I'm sorry, Lissie—" she cries. "Sit down and eat."

"I'll miss the bus, Mom—"

Dammit—my father says. *Dammit*—

"I'm only human," she says.

She composes herself. She's been reading a new book about Transcendental Meditation; she is wearing a mood ring that is stuck on orange, the color of anger. She takes three deep breaths.

"Forgive me, honey?" she says, looking down at me. "We're all adults, and adults make mistakes. But that *outfit* . . . I am going to *die*."

There are tears and screaming and cold washcloths pressed against swollen eyes.

"This is *not* how mothers and daughters behave," my father says to her, putting his coat on.

"Don't you dress her like a *boy!*" she screams back at him. "For *spite* you do it!"

. . .

IN THE FIFTH GRADE, I have become a woman.

"Just like me!" my mother says. She proudly points to herself, thumbs to her chest, while I step behind her, apoplectic with shame. She tells anyone who will listen—a neighbor, a stranger on line at the dry cleaner or the bank, the grocery man whose Holocaust survivor wife has a number tattooed on her arm in green ink.

A *minhag*: a Jewish custom without reason.

She slaps me on a bright Sunday morning after finding blood on my sheets. Gaga did it to her, and Gaga's mother did it to Gaga. No one knows why. It comes as a surprise: a sucker punch. I weep ugly tears that make my eyebrows swell. She grabs me in a loose hug. I hang limp as a ragdoll.

"Oh, darling, *stop crying* already! You're a *woman* now! Think of the boys—"

She shoves into my arms a small box of adhesive minipads that she has stashed under the sink in her bathroom; she has been waiting for just this occasion.

"Don't tell Dad—*please*, Ma—"

"*Cy!* She's a *woman*—" she yells, and my father races out of the bathroom wrapped in a damp towel, half his face covered with a meringue of Barbasol. He wraps his arms around me.

"Mazel tov, my beautiful girl—I'm so proud of you," he whispers in my ear, as though bleeding is an extraordinary feat at which a young girl might succeed or fail.

I am able to produce babies at eleven years old. I am no longer the bony, narrow child my mother used to lovingly shake into her tights like a pillow every morning before school, the one who she was sure would grow up to be tall and lanky and cool: her clone. I hear the words *zaftig* and *busty* spoken in low whispers around me. *The Life Cycle Library* shows up gift-wrapped in my bedroom, sitting on my dresser. The card says *Ask me anything, I'm here for you, Love Papa.*

May the tribe increase! he proclaims at the end of a family dinner at his sister's house on Long Island, twenty of us seated around my aunt's formal mahogany dining room table. My mother snorts and rolls her eyes; she gets up and excuses herself. My premature puberty is cause for public celebration; there will now be plenty of time for me to have babies. My shape, suddenly round and fertile and so very different from my mother's ectomorphic skeleton, becomes a topic of conversation; a punch line.

"Well," my father says when I try out for the local swim team, "at least you'll never drown."

"You're the *lucky* one," my mother says, sitting on my bed and watching me change into my play clothes after school. A ribbed turtleneck and brown corduroy jeans lie in a pile at my feet; I'm wearing nothing but a training bra and days-of-the-week underpants. She gets up and gently pushes a strand of hair out of my eyes; she puts her arms around me and we stare together like best friends, side by side, into the mirror.

"*You* got what the men want," she laughs, "not what *I* got. Flat as a goddamned pancake. Just *look* at me. Tits like yours and I could rule the world."

"But I don't want to rule the world," I say.

"You *will*," she says.

My mother poses with her hands in the belt loops of her

hip-huggers. She turns to the side, gazes over one shoulder and sucks in her cheeks, thin as a reed.

. . .

ON THIS SCHOOL MORNING IN 1974, I have dressed myself in a very special suit that my father has brought home from the city. One day after work, he secretly carried a black vinyl garment bag into my bedroom and hung it up in my closet before my mother could find it. My father believes that boys' clothes are made better, and will last longer, than girls', and he slips them into my wardrobe quietly, subversively, when my mother isn't looking. Severe and angular with massive pointed lapels, my new suit is fashioned from heavy English tweed of the sort that might be worn while walking on the moors with a dog and some sheep. It quietly thrills me, and when I pull it out of the closet, reaching past the technicolor dresses and the suede miniskirt and the rabbit fur vest, I am delighted; it is a small coat of armor and I wear it as though I am heading into battle. I use the bathroom, leave the bag of makeup samples on the sink, dry my hands, and button my jacket. I stuff my books into the heavy black belting leather briefcase that my father has also bought for me, the kind a middle-aged actuary might use, a utilitarian nineteen-fifties remnant acquired at a dusty midtown luggage store. Dressed like this, I will have a good day, I think; a safe day. I come down the hallway for breakfast.

"That's a man's bag, honey—" my mother notes, as I drag my briefcase into the kitchen.

"—leave it," she adds, taking a drag off her cigarette.

I let go of the handle.

"Take it," my father says, putting the newspaper down and climbing off the kitchen stool.

I pick it up.

"*Drop* it, Elissa," my mother says, shaking her head. "You're a lady. Not for you."

I look at them: My father is wearing a dark gray pinstriped suit, a striped tie, and brown horn-rimmed glasses. His initials are embroidered on his shirt cuffs in block letters. My mother, who won't return to work for another year, is dressed in brown suede lace-front hip-hugger bell-bottoms bought when we were in Monterey a few years earlier. Her silk blouse is gathered at the bottom and tied into a knot just above her navel. She is wearing heavy carved Mexican silver earrings. Her broken mood ring. Thick, opaque makeup. She sighs and shakes her head. The weight of the universe is kneeling on her shoulders. There is screaming; I stick my fingers in my ears. I make out the words *undertaker* and *whore*. Spatula, clock, floor.

"You are *not* a boy," my mother says to me. "Go back to your room and change into the clothes I bought you. Take off that suit—and enough with the briefcase."

"But—" I start.

"*Now—*"

I go back to my bedroom and start over. I lay the suit over the back of my desk chair. I take out black tights, a short flowered dress, tan suede cork-bottomed platform sandals. Like an apparition, I lean against my dresser and watch myself put the outfit on: first the tights, one leg and then the other, and then the dress. I buckle my sandals, which my mother says will give me a little height.

"Just *look* at you," she says, waving to me as I head down the hallway to the elevator with my father. "Beautiful! Walk in with your right foot!"

I climb the steps of the school bus with my books and my lunchbox. Our neighborhood flashes by in a blur: grocery store, bank, laundromat. When we arrive at school, my best friend nudges me.

"We're here," she says. "Let's go."

On a recent Saturday afternoon while my mother is having her hair done at Vidal Sassoon, my father and I step out of La Côte Basque, where I have been introduced to Coquilles Saint-Jacques and Sole Meunière. During lunch, he has instructed the waiter to bring me an empty shot glass into which he pours a drop of Burgundy, which burns the back of my throat. Most Saturdays of my childhood, this is what we do, in different restaurants all over Manhattan. Le Pavillon, La Grenouille, Le Périgord, the Praha. This is our time, and I wait for it all week. He teaches me about pleasure and flavor and sustenance. *Just between us,* he says. A clandestine adventure, a secret culinary affair that will end with my father flicking crumbs off my outfit with a glove compartment lint roller so that my mother, who believes that food is fuel and wants neither a fat husband nor a fat child, will never know where we've been.

My father and I leave La Côte Basque to find that the temperature has plunged thirty degrees. We walk three long, frigid blocks to Saks Fifth Avenue. We ride the escalator to the boys' department, where my father buys me a wool-lined Burberry-style trench coat that grazes my ankles. He has the clerk remove the tags—a frisson of danger ripples through me—flips up the broad tan gabardine collar, and buttons the scratchy neck guard across my throat.

"Just like *Ingrid Bergman*," he says as he ties my belt, bent down on one knee.

My mother sees me through the glass window of the salon where we pick her up. She smiles and waves like a starlet in the Rose Parade. We smile and wave back. We get closer and she sees my new coat. Her face drops as though she's had a stroke.

We ride home in silence. She slams their bedroom door so hard that yellow paint chips fly off the frame and through the air like confetti.

The following Monday, my mother picks me up from school, which she never does unless someone has died. I step out of the building and there she is, waiting outside, straining to find me. She spots me coming down the steps and waves.

"Who died?" I ask.

"We're going shopping today, sweetheart."

"Why?"

"Because you need some new things."

We ride the subway to the Fifty-Ninth Street basement station at Bloomingdale's. My mother chooses a pile of jewel-toned shirred cotton tube tops and a selection of transparent voile blouses to wear over them. My back turned to my mother, I stand in a dressing room in Levi's and Pro Keds and my Teen-form bra. I step into a tube top the color of burnt sienna, first one foot then the other. I pull it over my hips like a sausage casing.

"Over your *head*," my mother groans, "but you have to take off your bra first. What is *wrong* with you?"

I turn my back to her. My breasts are almost as large as hers.

She rolls her eyes. *Forgoddsake.* How is it possible, she wonders, that this girl—this daughter of a model, of a television star—doesn't know how to dress? How is it possible that this child is even related to her?

"Can you maybe at least *smile?*" she asks. "Can you just do that *for me?*"

I stare blankly into the mirror. I grin.

"Let's stop here—I need a mascara," she says on our way out of the store, slowing down in front of a wall of makeup mirrors. The crowd bustles around me; a perfume hawker sprays me with Charlie.

"Can I help you?" a tall, dark-haired clerk says.

"A makeover," my mother says, giving me a gentle nudge forward. "My daughter needs a little help."

The clerk looks down at me. I stand still, frozen, my hands stuffed into my jeans pockets.

"It'll be fun, honey—" my mother says. She is beaming; she is happy.

A makeover: to take what exists and make it over. A do-over. The fixing of a mistake.

The clerk comes out from behind the counter, bends down, and tells me to close my eyes. She applies three layers of shadow—a smoky gray *for allure,* she says; navy blue mascara and pink frosted lipstick, which matches the welts that erupt in a line along my jaw and down my neck. She turns me around to face my mother.

"Just *look* at you," my mother gasps.

She stands behind me and beams. She taps her chin— *Hold your head up,* it means—and hands me a mirror. I stare back at this small stranger, her eyes encircled by a mottling of dark color, like she's been in a street fight.

"*This* is how you should look," she squeals. "Can't you even *see yourself*? What's *wrong* with you? Can't you *see* the difference? Everyone says we look the same!"

"Like *sisters!*" says the salesgirl.

I gaze at the mirror. A round, spotty face gazes back at me, unrecognizable. It is expressionless. It feels embalmed, fake, like a made-up corpse. It appears to be wearing my hair.

My mother emits joy like a beam from a lighthouse. I have become a smaller version of her. On this school day afternoon in Manhattan in the midseventies, the things that give meaning and order to her life might now be mine too. She believes she has captivated and caught me, like a fish with a baited hook. I, her young daughter, will finally understand her. Love exists, pure and primal, but the affection between us, fleeting as a breeze, will finally be ours.

"Just *look* at you," she cries. "*Look—*"

She pulls me to her chest and hugs me tightly; she kisses the top of my head, stands back, and tips my chin up. My heart cracks open with joy.

3

SUSAN AND I ARE DRAWN TO THE FURY AND THE CALM OF MAINE, to the granite beach and the metal sky, and the straight-lined vernacular of assurance.

After my parents' divorce, my father and I spent our vacations together in rural Vermont. When he died in 2002, I began to search for him where we'd stayed so many years earlier, as though his essence might still exist in the places he loved. This seemed natural; the healing aspect of the Vermont hills drew me back, and Susan and I lived for a few weeks each autumn in a small, rustic cabin on Lake Dunmore outside Middlebury. It was our dog's vacation, we would tell people, and she would be wet and stinking from lake water from sunup to sundown. We would do little else but read, hike, cook, make love.

When Susan's mother died a few days before her ninety-

fifth birthday, we shifted our gaze even farther north, to where
the water was colder, the residents more taciturn, and life more
challenging. This shift happened organically; it was not something we discussed. Her mother had been a difficult but
generous-hearted woman, devoutly Catholic and deeply suspicious of anyone who wasn't. Prone to severe anxiety, she was
the daughter of a subsistence farmer and a stalwart, chary New
Englander morally opposed to frivolity or excess of any kind.

I love you like my own, she said to me when I cooked for her
one late winter afternoon, after she'd gotten sick. It came out
flat and hard, a statement of fact, cool as steel, without physical
contact. Our relationship had at turns been difficult and good,
black and white, hot and cold, a dance of patience and reticence. I had recently taken to calling her in the afternoons on
breaks from my work, to share with her good news or bad, to
talk about Susan and our garden, our successes and our fail-
ures. After surviving cancer twice two decades apart, her heart
had begun to slow. Where she had once spent afternoons on a
step ladder trimming an eight-foot hemlock hedge, she could
now barely water her flowers. I drove up one day to make her a
roast chicken; I cooked it in her old cast-iron Griswold skillet,
which had belonged to her late mother.

I love you like my own.

My knees weakened. She went to put a log on her fire.

In the same way Vermont comforted me when my father
died, Maine offered solace in the familiar when we lost Helen;
its contradictions of harshness and relief seemed recognizable.
*We shake with joy, we shake with grief, What a time they have,
these two, housed as they are in the same body,* wrote Mary Oli-
ver, and we came to Maine in part for this reason: The beauti-

ful and the dangerous—the gingerbread cottages; the deadly undertow—exist side by side.

One is not readily accepted in Maine, where people are politely designated as being either locals or from away. It can take generations of dwelling full-time in this formidable place—the literal ends of the earth that jut out into the violent north Atlantic like a hat hanging from a hook—before one is considered a native, and it is this fact that keeps us returning year after year: consistency breeds hope. *Come back, this place welcomes you,* our local friends say, in an invitation to community that is as sweet as honey. Susan and I look at real estate. We study coastal maps. We read Thoreau's *The Maine Woods* and the stories of Robert Tristram Coffin. A tide chart is folded into the small brown leather pocket notebook I carry everywhere, and although I have never been a sailor and grow ill at the first hint of choppy water, I learn to read it for reasons that have more to do with safety than affect. Artifice, perhaps, but we don't want to be caught off guard, unprepared. Susan and I, together almost two decades and peering over the edge of the third part of our lives, return to Maine for increasingly longer periods.

As we get older, our compass is pointing north.

. . .

WE FIRST SET EYES ON each other in the spring of 1986, but Susan and I would not meet for another fourteen years. It was after work on a warm day in the middle of Heckscher Field in the heart of Central Park when I first saw her: She had a long braid so inky black that in the right light it looked blue, pulled through the plastic adjusting tab on her baseball cap. She wore massive round, red English schoolboy glasses and a heavy neoprene pad encasing each knee, both of which had been injured over the years. While her teammates laughed and caroused around her, she stood in a ready position, waiting for the ball, all business, wanting no surprises. The six softball fields backed up onto each other; one team's infield was another's outfield. Players were regularly hit by stray fly balls. It was nervous-making and distracting, but Susan was focused, calm, and completely unfazed by the activity; her stillness in a sea of mayhem made her stand out, and I couldn't take my eyes off her.

"Don't hit to her," the captain of our team warned, but I did, and this woman in the ridiculous knee pads and funky glasses threw me out seconds after my feet left home plate.

We didn't say a word to each other. When the game was over and we all went out to drink at Dublin House, an Irish bar near Broadway, Susan went home to Brooklyn, where she was living in a long-term relationship with a woman, a Gestalt therapist she'd met years earlier. I was living on the Upper West Side with my mother and Ben, her second husband, a furrier, whom I loved. I went home to where he was likely still in his Hermès tie and work trousers, stretched out on the den sofa in front of the television with a Scotch in his hand. My mother, I imagine, stood over him, shouting about something—his children? money? dinner plans?—that the glow of alcohol would dull and soften, like a pillow over his head. A new canister of black fishnet stockings might have been waiting for me on the marble entryway table, and she might have pointed it out as I dropped my bags and took off my jacket.

We needed them, darling, so I bought a bunch, she might have said to me, taking a drag from her cigarette.

. . .

TWO DECADES LATER, WHILE SITTING on her couch, Susan will show me an old picture of herself during her softball days.

You're her, I said.

Susan's face had stayed with me all those years: the quiet woman in the field, focused and calm in the midst of trouble.

We met on a bitterly cold afternoon at the end of January 2000, the first month of the new millennium and the predicted apocalypse. Y2K had stopped neither time nor traffic, and we emailed back and forth for three months. Single for years, I had come to a fork in the road; I wrote a personal ad and put it up on an AOL message board. Susan answered it, one of two hundred responders. My finger hung over the Delete key for a full minute before I decided to open and read her note. On our first date, we ate Boeuf Bourguignon at a small country French restaurant in Greenwich Village and drank a bottle of rustic red wine. We shared our concerns: We lived two hours apart, and there would be commuting. She was ten years older than I, and that worried her. Her cell phone vibrated three times in the few hours we'd been together; I guessed, and I was right, that it was a girlfriend unconvinced that their relationship had ended two years earlier. Susan was very quiet, she said, and nobody seemed to like that much.

We talked about her mother's anxiety disorder so severe that she would spend her life never venturing more than twenty miles from her northern Connecticut home, and expecting Susan to do the same. My mother could be charming and tempestuous in a flash—predictable in her unpredictability—and had never known me as part of a couple nor ever seen me in love. I had been alone for a decade.

She's a problem, I said.

So is mine, Susan answered.

We went our separate ways for the night and met again the next day; we spent four hours eating brunch at a Polish restaurant in the East Village—butter-fried pierogi stuffed with potatoes and onions the color of mahogany; a long rope of gamy boiled kielbasa and spicy mustard that made me sneeze and my eyes run; scrambled eggs as soft as pillows—before Susan reached across the table out of a long silence, moved a black plastic basket of rolls aside, and touched a tiny scar on my right hand.

I was in the sixth grade and accidentally put my hand through an interior door window at school. My mother, who had recently gone back to work, couldn't be found. When I passed out in the school principal's office from blood loss—although the wound was very small, I had managed to nick an artery—there was no one to call. I waited in the nurse's office until the end of the day and, gray and wobbly, was sent home on the school bus with my friends. I came down the stairs at our bus stop with my bandaged hand stuffed deep in my coat

so as not to upset Gaga, my grandmother, who was waiting for
me in my mother's stead.

"How did you notice it?" I asked.

"How could I not?" Susan said.

A week later, the train trip to her tiny house in rural northern Connecticut took hours. We collapsed into each other's
arms and made love for three days, stopping only to let her dog
out. We called our mothers by cell and lied: *away on business,
an emergency project.* We fell asleep wrapped around each
other. I woke early and watched her.

I measure the accretion of time by the age of the baby we never
had, the number of older people we've lost, the cancer scares,
the boxes of inherited photos stacked up in our closet, the flut-
ter I get in my heart when I look across the table at her.

Nineteen years; long enough for us to have a child in college.

Nineteen years; I still wake before she does.

I take stock of her: the way her hair, once prematurely salt-
and-pepper, has now gone white in spots, and how quiet her
dreams are. When we're in Maine, our place of peace and par-
adox, I watch her in the quiet of the early mornings before my
mother calls, before our day begins, afraid of losing this love.

4

SEVEN EIGHTEEN A.M.; THE PHONE RINGS.

"What's doin', honey," she says, chewing something. "How's your hair?"

"Still attached," I say, flipping through her stack of business envelopes like a deck of playing cards. They are addressed to her, sent to my care.

"Is it big and beautiful?"

"It's fine, Ma—"

I take a sip of coffee.

She needs to be needed, a therapist friend once said.

Years ago, grasping for a shred of intimacy, I had told her the truth: My hair, heavy and curly and so thick it was often impossible to brush, suddenly seemed to be falling out in clumps. After I moved home from college and into her apartment, a cortisol overload—a rush of daily anxiety that flowed hot and angry like a geyser from the center of my belly—kept me awake morning and night.

You're in adrenal depletion, an East Village massage therapist told me, laying a lavender-soaked cotton chamois over my face. I tried everything to calm myself: valerian root that stank like dirty socks, two-in-the-morning wine in massive goblets that I hid in my mother's den closet at the foot of the pullout sofa where I slept. Chronic anxiety had blown out my endocrine system, thinning out the masses of my blond, uncontrollable curls that she loved.

Our crowning glory, she had called it, as if it belonged to both of us.

I took her out for lunch and asked her for her advice: It was a cosmetic issue, a problem of beauty, I reasoned, and she would know the answer. She would help me. It would bring us together.

"You're doing it on purpose because you *hate me,*" she bellowed from the waiting room of a specialist she'd found through her best friend, Lucille. He injected my twenty-five-year-old scalp with an expensive cure that turned out to be nothing more than saline solution, while two nurses blockaded the procedure room.

"I'll bring in a policeman if you don't let me in!" she screamed.

Any stress in your life? the doctor asked, as he hovered over me with a long syringe.

So all these years later: *Fine.* The hair is just fine.

Still, it is touching: that moments after waking, after her first cup of hot water and the fork scrapings of a day-old chicken breast draped under a sheet of plastic wrap in her fridge, my mother, frail from nearly a century of starving herself, would fret and keen over how I look. Because if I look different from her, if I *am* different from her, I will have abandoned her.

I'm exhausted with worry, she will say on those mornings. *I had to take a Xanax because of you.*

"What else is doin'? How's the dog?"

"Fine," I say. "He's fine."

"Does he need anything? Any toys? I could send him a toy—"

"The dog's *fine,* Ma—he doesn't need anything—"

"Something new—I'll go to the drugstore. They have dog toys—"

"He's *fine,* Mom—please—"

The dog has fallen in love with my mother, and she with him. Petey is a scruffy apricot-colored mutt of indeterminate origin, a herder who was rescued from a Memphis ditch when he was three months old. He arrived at our Connecticut home a month later not knowing what to do with toys and unable to smile or wag. Not interested in food, he couldn't be trained with treats; he was traumatized and distrustful, hardwired for survival. Susan and I worried about what and who he would become: Would he accept love and grow into his own heart? Or would he remain snappish and unpredictable?

What happened to him, this darling baby, my mother asked when they first met, pulling him into her lap and squeezing his neck. He fought her but never growled, squirming to get away until she forced his twenty pounds into place; he gave up and went limp as a corpse, and she showered his yellow head with kisses that left red Clinique lipstick stains from his ears to his eyebrows like a tattoo.

My mother prefers dogs to people; she trusts them more, she says, and I grew up loving them as much as she does. It was learned behavior.

Dogs will never turn on you, she said, *provided you give them love and affection, and sometimes even if you don't.* When we walk in Manhattan, we will stop and say hello to whoever approaches us, regardless of size: drooling Newfoundlands, snorting pugs, bounding golden retrievers, teacup poodles. She introduces herself to the animals but never to their people, bending down, taking their heads in her hands, stroking them. I come by my love of dogs honestly; they were not clean or predictable enough for my father, who merely tolerated them. I get my affection for animals purely and solely from her, a shared affinity for these wordless creatures of ritual and joy who are often left behind like garbage, who only ever want the simplest of kindnesses.

When she visits, she showers Petey with gifts; he won't leave her side. He follows her to the bathroom and into the guest room; he sleeps on the bed next to her. One late weekend afternoon, I furtively filmed her over her shoulder while she sat on our living room loveseat with him. Susan and I were in the kitchen, cooking, and my mother removed a slender antique volume from our bookshelf—how did she come to choose it?—and I could hear her reading him *Moldy Warp the Mole,* an English children's book. Petey's head rested in her lap, his eyes closed. She stroked him gently, like a baby.

———

On our early-morning call, after we've covered my hair, and Petey, and his need for more toys, my mother asks, "And how is *she?*"

"Fine—" I say "—and her name is Susan."

"You *always* want to fight—" she says, sighing.

After nineteen years, the fact of Susan is an irritant to my mother, like lemon in a paper cut.

"She never expected you two to last so long," Lucille, my mother's best friend, once told me.

A fact-finding mission. I called her one night after ten years of being out of touch. I reached out to her out of the blue, adult to adult, to get a sense of perspective: She'd known my mother for sixty years. But Lucille and my mother were no longer speaking; they fought about money and men and my mother's bottomless fount of need and desire. My mother told her she was entitled to have whatever she wanted because she'd given up so much. Lucille told my mother to see a psychiatrist.

"You're a cunt, Zelnick," my mother told her, and said good-bye forever.

I sat on the couch with a glass of Scotch and listened to Lucille's hard-edged Brooklyn whine. She had known my mother early on while she was on television. I dug around my mother's life that night like a miner with a pickax, looking for the edges of our narrative, the ecotones, trying to fit our story together and make sense of it. I searched for the corners, the anchors, and the foundation like the pieces of the jigsaw puzzle we assemble every year at the Maine house.

"She thought your father had money," Lucille said, "and he didn't. She thought she'd be a star again, and she wasn't. She thought you'd be just like her, and you aren't. She thought a man would always be there to take care of her, and she was wrong. Your mother is not a woman equipped for disappointment . . ."

I listened.

". . . and she blames Susan for everything, for taking you away from her, for making you leave the city. You could be giving to her what you're giving to your wife. I'm sorry, sweetheart."

A chill crawled up my spine, the kind that comes with the onset of flu.

"What *is* it?" my mother asks during our call. "I can hear it in your voice—it's *something.*"

I flip through the pile of bills and statements rubber-banded on the table in front of me. She's run short again; something's gone haywire. *A bad month,* she says. I can always quietly help tide her over. Sometimes she won't even notice it. We don't have to talk about it. Money often appears, miraculously, in her account; a gift from the gods. We can simply avoid the conversation. We can talk about the dog.

But artists' lives are feast or famine. When things break— a printer, a tooth, a muffler—they sometimes stay broken until Susan and I can afford to fix them. If I am my mother's keeper— the person who makes sure that, in older age, her practical needs are addressed and met, and who assures her safety— I should know the truth. It is only right; I rationalize this. I ask her the way a parent asks their teenager about the sudden appearance of a dent in the family car.

"Mom," I say gently. "Is there something you want to tell me?"

Silence.

"I had to buy food," she says. "I *must* eat—would you rather I starve to death and die?"

She turns up the television volume so we can't hear each other. I shout over Ilsa and Rick. *The Germans wore gray; you wore blue.*

"You have nothing in your fridge. I checked the other day."

On the first of my twice-monthly visits, I opened her refrigerator for a quick inspection. A pint of matzo ball soup. A roast turkey leg. Slices of rye bread and bags of pickles from the local deli. Ancient Milk of Magnesia. Last year's bottle of Pinot Grigio that sits in the door, open and corkless, its thin green neck stuffed with a wad of tin foil.

"If you're not buying food, Ma, where's the money going?"

"I don't have to tell you *anything*," she growls. "It's none of your goddamned business. Even Dick says I don't have to tell you."

She has met a younger man.

I like to be seen with you on my arm, he has told her.

She coos when she talks about him; she bats her eyelashes, like a silent-movie actress.

Susan and I are pleased. We would like her to meet someone who can give her the attention she craves, someone who can fill the need bucket, unlike the psychiatrist a decade earlier whom she gifted with half a dozen Hermès scarves in their flat orange boxes and who ended their working relationship when she demanded he leave his wife for her. We wonder whether this new man is really interested in her or she's imagining it, the way she once believed she was dating Paul, her musical accompanist.

"He's gay, Mom," I told her. "He lives with his husband."

"I could change him," she said. "He just needs a good woman."

Dick is six years older than I, tall and doughy, pale as a potato, and spends his days gambling in Atlantic City since his wife recently died, tragically young, not yet fifty. I compare him to Ben the furrier, whom she married the summer before I left for college: natty, funny, kind Ben. Ben with the heart of gold and the patience of Job, who covered her in the important jewelry that she loved: the massive pieces engorged with square-cut, large-carat diamonds and emeralds that made people gasp and worry for her safety as she walked from one side of the city to the other. Ben, whose grown children and grandchildren she refused to let into the house because she was certain they stole. Ben, who slowly drank himself to death in front of *The Cosby Show* every night when they got home from work. He died of a cerebral hemorrhage, which my mother was certain was an allergic reaction to the shrimp and lobster sauce they'd ordered from Empire Szechuan on Seventy-Second Street.

An all-er-gy, she wept to the triage nurse when I found her on that rain-soaked January night in 1997, drenched to the skin and sitting alone in the busy emergency room at Mount Sinai, long tracks of black mascara running down the sides of her face. *Nothing but an all-er-gy.*

"Dick is a *very* fine man," she says on our morning call, her voice deep and furious. "You just want me to be alone. *I know.* You're just jealous, because I have Dick and you don't."

"I'm a lesbian, Mom. I don't want Dick."

"I have no food in the house—none. So I took some money out, and for this you're yelling at me? Don't send me a birthday present this year. I'd rather have the cash."

"I'll send you food, Ma," I say, "but not cash."

"I did for *you!*" she screams, "and now *you* do for *me*. You have *no* idea what I gave up for you—you don't even *know*."

"So tell me, Ma," I say, sipping my coffee. "I'm listening."

"Your grandmother walked out on your father when he was a baby and he *still* gave her everything she ever wanted. He gave her what should have been *mine*—She left her family—I *never* left—"

For reasons long forgotten or perhaps never known, my paternal grandmother, nearly one hundred years ago and at the age of twenty-four, walked out on her husband, three-year-old son, and young daughter and took up with a man of vague wealth and shady pedigree. Unable to reconcile her bourgeois desires with her bohemian lust, this tiny Romanian immigrant who arrived on Ellis Island as a toddler in steerage fell for the man's promises of things that would change her place in the world and its perception of her: a yacht, a motorcar, trips to Paris, furs.

His mother's leaving was my father's weak point—the loose brick in his wall—the spot that, when attacked, made him crumble like strudel. He was a little boy; for three years he prayed for her return, and after three years of my grandfather's begging she came home. All was forgiven. Rife with desperation and abandonment, the story became the foundation upon which my father's life was built; one part of his family hid it for fifty years. It became corrosive; shame engulfed generation after generation.

As a child, I suffer from profound separation anxiety. I am certain that my mother will go grocery shopping and never return. She'll have her hair done and disappear. She'll take a taxi to the state line. These things happen. Famous: Doris Lessing walks out on her two eldest children and husband in Rhodesia and moves to London so that she can have a literary career, believing that motherhood and the making of art are mutually exclusive. Not famous: my stocky Jewish grandmother from the old country leaves her children and husband at the start of the Depression.

In our family, it never mattered that my grandmother came back. That wasn't the point. In her twenties, believing that her life would not be fulfilled if she stayed, she had the will and the inclination to leave. And she did.

But is there *more*? Is there a part of her story that no one knows, that none of us could possibly imagine, that we can only guess at? A young mother, small and beautiful, of Orthodox Jewish lineage, bore her husband two children, a boy and a girl, five years apart. She was kind and warm. She cleaned house and made sure her children were washed and dressed and her husband satisfied. She cooked for her family every morning and every night, and cared for her own aging mother, who lived over the bridge in lower Manhattan. And this is where things go murky. Had my father's mother been filled with some sort of visceral regret that tore her apart? Was her husband violent? Did she suffer from postpartum depression?

Did my grandmother run away to save herself?

Walking out: indefensible.

The stamp of abandonment was imprinted on our little family like a wax seal. My mother became obsessed: The story wormed its way into every conversation, every spat, every dis-agreement. She would pull out this nugget of shame midfight, like a switchblade from a back pocket, and hurl it at my father's head across the table over the Friday night brisket and the Soave.

Your mother left; your mother walked out; your mother didn't love you.

My father, red-faced and trembling, would stand up, put the leash on the dog, and walk him into the Queens night.

On this, our daily morning call, after she asks about my hair and my dog and my wife and I ask her where her money is going, I want her to tell me what she gave up.

"Everything," she says, her voice breaking. "I gave up *every-thing* for you, because I love you—"

"Tell me, Mom—"

"Already—*this* is what you're doing to me?" she shrieks.

I set the phone down on the dining room table next to the envelopes. I press Talk so she can't call me back. I sit on the sofa and throw the pillows on the floor. I wrap my arms around my knees.

Seven twenty-six A.M.

Streaks of light brighten the living room. The sun is com-ing up.

A new morning; a new day.

5

NEW YORK HOSPITAL.

We go there because, fifty-two years ago, that's where I was born. We go there because my mother believes that every other hospital in Manhattan is a suspect, filthy repository of syphilitics where people go in and never come out.

It's an early Saturday night in December 2016. I am home from a long book tour. It's the first night in weeks that Susan and I are together; it's quiet in the house. We've built a fire. We've opened a good bottle of Pinot Noir. We're reheating a block of frozen turkey soup left over from Thanksgiving, a month earlier.

Every holiday my mother says *Just make a reservation* and I say *No, I want to cook. I want my family around my table. I*

am convinced of it: Our table—handmade by a local crafts-
man from three-hundred-fifty-year-old New Hampshire wormy
maple barnwood, and alive with history—will save us. We will
sit down together around antique ironstone platters laden with
foods that my mother will consume with delight, and like Clark
Kent in a phone booth, she will magically morph into Mother
Walton. Peace will be ours.

Living out my Rockwellian Thanksgiving fantasy, I corral
every stray person I know to avoid having it just be the three of
us—me, Susan, my mother—because just the three of us is
grim. Three of us might as well be watching the parade in front
of the television and eating Swanson's frozen turkey dinners
with the little apple crisp in the middle of the aluminum tray.
Three of us is my culinary PTSD trigger. It sends me hurtling
back to the first Thanksgiving after my parents' divorce in
1978, when Gaga, wanting the holiday to be exactly the same
as it had been in the past, roasted a twenty-pound Butterball
and made her baked sweet potatoes and cornflake pie topped
with marshmallows. The turkey emerged from the oven, she
and I carried it over to the dining room table on an orange
melamine platter, and my mother said, *What the hell do we do
now.* At fifteen years old, I pulled from the drawer an old serrated bread knife left behind by my father in his haste to flee
and dismembered the bird over the course of an hour, sawing
and pulling, chopping and slashing, until it was a pile of shredded, dry meat with the consistency of balsa wood. My mother,
chewing on the leathery tip of a wing, turned on the little television set that sat like a dinner guest at the end of the table and
watched *Gone with the Wind,* mouthing all of Scarlett O'Hara's
lines and *That Vivien Leigh was such a whore.*

Avoiding *the three of us,* Susan and I invite a close friend—single father, recently divorced, a practicing Quaker—and his two little girls to join us for the holiday. They are vegetarians, and we have gone to lengths to cook extra dishes for them that they will enjoy. We have warned my mother far in advance of the day.

We have a friend coming with small children, we said a month earlier.

My mother's face grew sour when we told her; her lips curled down in despair. My stomach dropped.

Why, she asked.

Because it's their first holiday alone, and we wanted them with us, I said.

But why, she asked.

Because they're our friends, I said.

But I'm your mother, she said.

On Thanksgiving, my mother steps out of the house as they pull in to the driveway in their red Prius, a bit dinged, covered in bumper stickers about Tibet and visualizing world peace. The car doors swing open and the little girls jump out excitedly, as little girls do. They throw their arms around me. I pick the little one up and she wraps her legs around my waist while my mother paces around the yard behind me.

"Don't they have a *mother* they can go to?"

"Ma," I say, spinning around.

"I don't understand why you feel the need to take everyone in, like stray dogs. What are you trying to prove? What have they done for you that *I* haven't done?"

She had been thinking about this for a month, ruminating on it, and lying in wait for the holiday to arrive.

I put the smaller girl down. At five and seven, they stand stock-still and unblinking, clutching threadbare stuffed animals to their chests. My mother sticks her tongue out at them. They simultaneously burst into tears. Their father takes them for a walk to visit the miniature horses at a farm down the street. Inside the house, our local heritage breed turkey, stuffed with long-fermented sourdough cubes and heirloom apples, its skin massaged with sweet butter churned from the creamy milk of nearby pastured Hereford cows, roasts to a burnished bronze.

"Get me a cab," my mother demands. "I *must* go home."

"I *can't* get you a cab. This is the country—and it's *Thanksgiving*—please, Mom."

"Find one," she growls. Her dark eyes go black and crazed; her mouth, twisted with fury, is set against her face growing paler with her anger and painted with a fierce red lipstick. She looks like Edobee, the eighteenth-century Kabuki warrior, menacing and malicious.

"Just calm down," I say. "Come inside. We'll have a nice dinner."

I'm still in my apron, splattered with turkey stock. I follow her around the front yard, pleading; she's strutting like a peacock, her back to me, struggling to release her black leather Miu Miu kitten heels, which get stuck in the lawn with every step.

"I want to go home," she says. "Or *they* have to leave. Don't you know how much I love you, honey? I did *not* raise you to act like this—"

Susan flies out of the house; the storm door slams behind her. She leaps off the top step of the porch and into the yard and grabs my mother by the lapels of her fur coat; bits of ancient sable float on the cool autumn air.

"*Behave* yourself, Rita," Susan says in a quiet, measured voice, "or you're going home."

"How dare you," my mother says, spitting with fury. "How *dare* you—Who the hell do you think you *are* to talk to me this way? I thought you were a *Buddhist.*"

"Call her a car," Susan says to me. "We'll pay anything. Just get her out of here."

My stomach falls; my neck is wet. Sweat drips in a thin line down the small of my back. I can't move my feet or feel my hands. *Come home with me,* my mother's wide, hysterical eyes say. *Come home to the city. You belong to me. We belong together.*

Two hundred dollars in cash transports my mother back to Manhattan on Thanksgiving Day.

"I didn't think you'd really do it—" she bellows when the Lincoln Town Car pulls in to our driveway. "So *thank* you very much. *I* am your mother."

The driver opens the door and helps her in. He offers her a bottle of water. Her mouth is still moving, she is still waving a finger at me so furiously that her charm bracelet rattles—*I'll fix you,* she shouts; *I'll fix you*—as he closes the door and she disappears behind the darkened window. They drive away.

Susan links arms with me and we go into our house. The children return from the walk with their father.

We sit down at the table with our friends. We give thanks. We eat.

———

A month later, on this December Saturday night after my book tour, the radio is tuned to *The Moth;* Susan and I sit on the couch together, the dog at our feet, listening to quiet stories that are mundane and funny and tragic. The theme is survival and rescue. The voices are calming, intimate. We've made love—tender, generous, late-afternoon winter love between two middle-aged people decades familiar with each other's bodies and their quirks: the aching left knee, the cramping foot, the torn rotator cuff, the inhibiting serotonin reuptake inhibitor. This is what we do, our routine, our home.

The leftover turkey soup is bubbling on the stove when the phone rings. I hesitate to answer; I look at Susan, whose eyes are half closed as she listens intently to the voices on the radio. I think about letting the call go to voicemail.

It had been the subject of a recent therapy session—my need to answer the phone, the inability to protect myself with a filter. The belief that whatever she was dishing out, I somehow deserved.

"Why do you always feel the need to answer?" my therapist asked. "Love doesn't mean you're available twenty-four hours a day. Where does that compulsion come from—to answer every call, to be responsible for her fury?"

"She might die—" I whispered.

"*You* might die," the therapist said. "An addiction. The belief that you have the power to ease her yearning—does it ever occur to you that she has you trained like a chimp?"

"You have me trained like a *chimp*," I cry when my mother calls again that night, the third time that day.

"I sung with a chimp once on television," she says. "His

name was Zippy. He wore a blue snowsuit and shoved his hand down my dress while we were live. My God, even *he* wanted me. He bit Arlene Francis the next week. Are you still on that diet?"

I stop answering all her calls, fourteen in one day when she was lonely and then sad and then happy and then enraged and she wanted to tell me everything, absolutely every single thing that happened to her, hour by hour, minute by minute. The bastard delivery boy from the deli brought her the wrong yogurt. The actors' club where she sings every Friday night wants her to open the show but she hates the accompanist and needs rehearsals, if only she had some extra money.

I get up from the couch and answer the call on the third ring. I drop the pitch of my voice as though it's armor protecting my vital organs. I never know who will be on the other end: Happy Rita, who has just been stopped on the street by someone wanting to take her picture because they saw her on a television show, they think, and she's not saying that she's not Iris Apfel—my mother's been wearing the glasses longer than Iris has—whom she hates because Iris is ninety and my mother is certainly not ninety. She might be pleasantly slurring Rita, asking after the dog. She might be furious Rita, hoping to fight, gloves off, demanding engagement and its addictive rush of endorphins.

"Lissie—*Lissie*—"

"Whut—"

She wheezes and pants and gasps.

Heart attack: the stopping of the engine, the breakdown of the motor that has propelled her through an unforgiving world that's done her wrong at every turn. With her cholesterol in the four hundreds and a bleak family history, I am sure that this is what will take her, the way it took Gaga.

"Darling—" she says. "Darling—my ankle is broke— *broke*—"

"*What?*"

"Broke—*please*—"

"Impossible," I say. "That can't be—"

My mother is immune to damage; she bounces like a rubber ball, she is unbreakable, unstoppable. She will live forever, and my job is to keep her whole, to keep her from exploding into pieces like a crystal globe dropped from a window.

There is no break, I decide.

"Please—" she cries. "*Please*—"

She is squealing like a baby; she is frightened, alone. It is a voice I've never heard.

. . .

"SHE WILL PROBABLY FALL," HER doctor told me months earlier, while my mother got dressed in the examination room down the hall.

We were no longer cautious about our conversations; the rules and limits about what a physician can say to an adult daughter whose older mother is not taking care of herself can be bent when that mother is in danger.

For years, my mother went to her appointments on her

own, picking and choosing what to share with both me and her physicians, editing out unnecessary details: her unhealthfully low weight, severe depression, the Parkinson's that blazes through our family like wildfire. There were crashing blood sugar problems for which she ate cheap bars of chocolate hidden half unwrapped in her purse, a wheat allergy ameliorated by twice-daily slices of white sandwich bread, hip pains for which she took a tiny orange antihistamine tablet strong enough to sedate an elephant, a troubling family cardiac history that she'd conveniently forgotten.

"So what did the doctor say?" I'd ask, calling her after her appointments.

"Oh, nothing—I stopped at Bergdorf on the way home for a lipstick."

"They couldn't have said *nothing*, Mom—"

"Everything is just *perfect*," she'd say, lightly. "Would you rather I be sick? I'm sure you would."

Magical thinking: I began to believe her, to believe that nothing would ever go wrong, simply because she was so beautiful. Apart from having a small cyst removed from her delicate collarbone, my mother was never once sick when I was a child: There were no flus, no colds, no infections, no stomach viruses or food poisonings, no cuts, no scrapes, no tumbles. Maladies large and small leaped a generation as though I had taken on the mantle of illness for both of us, carrying in my cells the imperfect, unattractive weight of affliction. I was unwell all the time, spiking dangerously high fevers with every sniffle. As a child, I terrorized her with my routine viruses to the degree that she simply could not bring herself to care for me. It was too upsetting; she loved me too much. She entrusted my nursing to my father and to an older woman who lived in our building, a medical technologist with a boutique practice in Manhattan. When I got sick as a teenager, my mother's remedy was to take me shopping, propping me up against the inside of dressing rooms all over the city, holding outfits up against me, imploring me to smile because it was impossible to be sick and beautiful at the same time. My mother's health—the fact of her aging, her living or dying—is bound up in her beauty, as if her looks themselves will protect her from the absolute inevitability of death.

If she stays beautiful, she will live forever.

"It will be a hip or a femur," her doctor told me while my mother got dressed in the room down the hall. A pleasant woman in her early fifties, she seemed weary in her white coat, stethoscope around her neck, a hint of crusting mascara on her glasses. Caring for older patients who would not—could not—come to terms with their own limitations weighed on her.

"She doesn't eat," she went on. "She's afraid of gaining weight. She's built like a bird. She says she's taking the osteo medication I gave her, but I don't think that's true. There's no change to her test results."

"*What* osteo medication?" I asked. "I didn't fill anything—"

Older people—even outlandishly stunning and impetuous ones who get stopped on the street by *Vogue* to have their photos taken, and who their children believe will simply never age—are regressive. Young children feed their vitamins to the family dog, slipping them under the table when they think no one is looking. Teenagers hide their indiscretions from their parents: A joint is flushed, school is cut, the family car borrowed for a joyride out of state, pills are filched from a medicine cabinet. Older people are no different: Lies are told, stories spun, promises broken. A neighbor's ninety-year-old father, restricted by his children and the state from driving, mows down a neighborhood mailbox and, in the process, an orange cat. A once-wealthy woman spends her money on cheap street jewelry and Vuitton knockoffs sold by Liberian refugees; penniless, she tells her daughter, who is supporting her, that they were gifts from her neighbor. A friend's mother, at eighty-five and suffering from vertigo, props her rusting metal extension ladder against the side of her two-story colonial and cleans her gutters; she tells her daughter that the boy next door did it, even though he's in Afghanistan on his second tour of duty. "He was on leave," she shrugs to her daughter, certain that her daughter will believe her.

These are not manifestations of dementia; these are mystical truths. Our lives are bound up in the vast human capacity for illusion, and older people believe that they are still the decision makers, the choosers, the planners, the ones in control. They are the same at ninety and eighty as they were at fifty.

"Osteo medication is for *old* people," my mother told the doctor. "I refuse to take it. And Dick says it will kill me."

"He's wrong," her doctor said. "*Not* taking it will kill you."

"He's not wrong," my mother said. "He's a man."

Her doctor wrote the prescription anyway and stuffed it into my mother's hand. She visited the bathroom, reapplied her lipstick, tore the prescription up, and threw it into the trash on her way out of the office, on her last visit without me.

"Did she give you anything new?" I asked when she got home.

"No," my mother lied. "Nothing at all. I stopped at Bergdorf."

Sitting on the floor of her den on the Upper West Side, propped against the new beige linen pullout sofa where we sleep when we visit, my mother drops the phone and passes out. She comes back for a minute and passes out again. At some point, she crawls into the bathroom, sheds her soiled robe and pajama bottoms like snakeskin, and slithers back to the bedroom. She passes out again.

It takes two hours to get from our house in northern Connecticut to her apartment, which is locked. No one else—not the doorman, the super, a neighbor, a friend, a cousin in Riverdale—has a key; it's a trust thing that dates back to the seventies, when New York City apartment break-ins were common. Unless we can get there quickly, an ambulance will have to remove the door, which is secured with three Israeli-made high-security locks installed by a man who used to work for the Mossad. The papers she will need for the hospital are buried amid old sheet music, press clippings, and bank statements, in half a dozen massive white plastic shopping bags left over from when she and Ben were furriers to the stars, thirty years earlier. Each bag is large enough to hold a king-sized down comforter; they are strewn all over the apartment as though they were picked up and flung around in a cyclone.

"Someday, my darling," she likes to say, "I will show you

where all the important things are. The good jewelry. Grand-pa's watch. The papers."

A rare acknowledgment of mortality, of the fact that life is finite and fixed, with a beginning and an end. There is no one else but me—I have no siblings, she has no siblings or spouse; there are no aunts or uncles or even friends anymore—and that at some point, I will be charged with her care and the settlement of her affairs. Someday, she will be gone.

"You're all I've got, my darling," she will say. "You're all there is."

On this December night, with her left ankle a pale blue explosion of softened bone and sinew and atrophied muscle, and her right fifth metatarsal splintered like a dry Popsicle stick, she waits for us, dazed and in shock. When we arrive, I discover I have left behind one of her keys on my entryway table; I can't get in. She drags herself half naked to the front door, reaches up from the floor as high as her thin, mottled arms will stretch, turns the doorknob, and collapses in a heap.

6

WHEN WE MET, SUSAN LIVED IN A TINY GRAY HALF-CAPE
twenty-five miles west of Hartford, set back from a narrow,
winding country road behind an unfinished picket fence. The
right size for one person and a dog, which at that time comprised Susan's immediate family—it was just she and McGil-
licuddy, a black curly-coated retriever with leaves in her fur
and unsure of her own canine status—the house stood at the
top of a hill overlooking a perfectly flat, sun-splashed acre of
land push-mowed twice weekly in the heat of the summer
by Susan's mother, Helen, who lived nearby and was, at the
time, eighty-two.

Susan's little house was filled with broad washes of light
and air. Heavy iron shoemaking forms once belonging to Susan's farmer grandmother, who handmade oxfords for the

twenty-two feet of her eleven children, propped open doors and the wide slider that led from the kitchen to the deck and down to the backyard. A square skylight was set into the roof directly above the bed we shared; a pair of rose-breasted grosbeaks sat on its edge one late afternoon and watched us sleep. A window behind the stove was perpetually in need of being cleaned of grease from the dinners that Susan cooked for herself in the house's perfectly square kitchen; it faced a massive 1930s three-bowl farmhouse sink above which hung a wide bookshelf housing old cookbooks from the sixties and seventies, including Susan's childhood copy of Julia Child's *Mastering the Art of French Cooking,* from which she produced for her mother and father Sole Mornay one night when she was twelve. At the right time of day, sun blazed through the house like a laser: the bed, the sink, the books were illuminated.

Susan came home to Connecticut after more than twenty years away, living first in brownstone Brooklyn and then in a sprawling eighteenth-century farmhouse in the countryside near Philadelphia.

"Why did you come back?" I asked her one night, not long after we met. There was no work in this part of northern Connecticut for a graphic designer. "Why didn't you stay where you were?"

"Because," she said, "my mother was getting older. I had come home for a visit, and she was too thin. She'd had cancer twice. She wasn't eating. I lived with her for two years before I bought this house."

Moral obligation; the dedication of daughter to mother; age and illness trump history.

There had been two mostly consecutive long-term relationships: one with Judy, an older Jewish Manhattan Gestalt therapist Susan had been with for thirteen years. And one with
Kathleen, a beautiful, dark-haired Irish American painter who
was not entirely convinced of her breakup with Susan, two
years after it happened.

"We loved Kathleen," Helen said to me one summer evening, while sipping a vodka tonic on Susan's deck. "She was so
funny, and so beautiful."

"And so Catholic," Susan added.

"Yes," Helen said. "That's right."

These were the two things that Susan assured me were of
key importance to her mother, a devout Catholic, and her mother's array of sisters, who all still lived in the area: beauty and devotion. There were Ethel, Sophie, Millie, Stephanie, and Phyllis,
who comprised a portion of the siblings born to Susan's grandmother, widowed at forty and left with eleven children shortly
after the end of World War I. Up and down the narrow hallway
that led from Susan's kitchen to the guest room hung a dozen old
family photographs framed in the ornate carvings of the times:
There are all the sisters and their mother, every one of them
blond and blue-eyed, together at a wedding. There are all the
young girls in prim white confirmation dresses, leaning up
against the family Model A, a spaniel running around at their
feet. There are the handsome, chiseled brothers in cutaway
morning suits and all the sisters in white fur stoles and a priest
lined up in a row from big to small, low to high. There are engagement photos and a formal Marine shot of Susan's father in

1943, and a picture of Helen in a long tweed skirt, standing on a rock protruding from a stream, looking away from the camera, fishing pole in hand.

There are only two pictures of Susan in her home. One is a professional studio portrait taken before her first birthday, six months after her adoption: Susan will often look like this, preoccupied, her attention cocked elsewhere, lost in thought, distrait. She gazes up at the camera, her gray-green eyes distracted by something out of frame, something we cannot see. In the other picture, taken at three years old, she is wearing a tiny dress, standing on the broad sill of a massive picture window at her aunt Millie's new house. She grasps for the disembodied feminine hand of a woman who reaches in to the shot to assure the child that she is not alone, that she is safe.

7

A PHOTO I HAVE NEVER SEEN BEFORE:

She is needle-thin, dressed in a short black shift with three-quarter sleeves. Her platinum pageboy is ironed straight. There are a charm bracelet, important wedding pearls, crossed legs, a cigarette in her hand. She gazes at the camera—my father's beloved Hasselblad, I reckon, and his treasure—with a shy, coy glance, a combination of yearning and resignation.

The red date stamp on the edge of the photograph says that it is 1962, September.

I imagine the traffic rattling by twenty-one stories below on First Avenue and Seventy-Ninth Street. My father's turntable plays Johnny Hodges and Billy Strayhorn's "Your Love Has Faded." My mother is pregnant—I was conceived on their wedding night, and there are the pearls—but these are the days long before maternal fret, back when there was no anxiety about smoking while carrying a baby. Hanging on the wall behind her is my father's ersatz Jackson Pollock, painted for him by the art director at his ad agency, where he is vice president of creative. If I close my eyes, I can feel the painting's bumps and rivulets of thick color that run down the canvas in heavy streaks, like blood.

My first memory, preverbal: I am being held over my mother's shoulder, so close to the massive canvas that even now, more than half a century later, the smell of acrylic paint sets off a primal response in me, like the first taste of sweetened milk touched to the tongue of an Italian newborn, which, they say, lingers until his last breath. From the time I am born in Manhattan in 1963 until we move to Forest Hills a year later, my mother will give me a bottle three times a day, measured perfectly to the ounce, no more, no less, and burp me against her husband's prized painting in quiet defiance.

. . .

THE NIGHT I FIND THIS photo, more than half a century after it was taken, my mother's accident is two years away. By day, she is still a flaneuse, traversing the city from east to west and north to south. Borders: She won't go below Twenty-Third Street or above Eighty-Sixth, lost in a pyschogeographic reverie that will take her in and out of bookstores and tchotchke shops, coffeehouses and small grocers, boutiques and jewelry stores and

Bergdorf Goodman. Here is Steinway Hall, where she per-
formed at fifteen. Here is the small independent bookstore
with the café that used to give her little squares of dark Belgian
chocolate for free—for *free!* she tells me, because they love
how she looks—and here is the Clinique kiosk at Bergdorf,
where they hoard samples for her to try because she buys so
much from them, spending hours there at least twice a week.

Every day, my mother, made up for the camera, will walk
and walk, dragging along a soft navy blue canvas tote bag badly
embellished with silver and red spangles sewn on in a slapdash
modern design. Long-handled and flaccid, the bag is filled with
necessities for the day: her makeup bag; a small zippered Vuitton key case in which are stuffed her identification, credit
cards, and cash; two copies of the CD she recorded in the late
nineties, along with a sheaf of her reviews from *Time Out New
York;* a few pieces of dog-eared sheet music for her favorite
songs transcribed into the key of B flat in the event that she is
called upon to perform; her cell phone; her tiny red leather
Filofax filled with scrawled-upon diary pages five years old; and
a small plastic bottle of water, its neck coated in fuchsia lipstick, as though she's shoved the entire thing into her mouth
like a baby who is just learning how to drink without a nipple.

My mother is ballasted by these essentials of life; all that
she could possibly need or want is carried with her each day on
her excursions. *Walking is mapping with your feet,* says Lauren
Elkin. It is how my mother locates herself in time and space. It
provides context, sets her down in the world, and organizes her
place in the center of it. When she arrives home, she is exhausted, not only from the five or six miles she has walked in

high heels with her navy canvas tote bag, but from the sheer drunkenness that comes from stimulus overload. The city is an assaultive drug, a high.

Why would you ever go? she asks when I leave New York to be with Susan. *And don't give me that I-moved-for-love garbage.*

The city is life, and where there is life, there can be no death. *Solvitur ambulando,* the Latin expression goes: *It is solved by walking.* And so, until her accident, she walks and walks; she solves and she lives.

I have driven in from Connecticut to take her out to dinner; she has spent the day on her feet and doesn't want to go far, so we eat at Café Luxembourg, our favorite bistro down the street from her apartment on the Upper West Side, where she has lived since marrying Ben in 1981. Her walk today has been truncated—she has fought with a friend, she is aggravated and tired—and so we don't go far.

"I'm so sad, Lissie darling," she says on this evening when I arrive at the apartment.

"I know you are, Mom," I say, "but you look so beautiful."

"Like *shit,* darling," she says, standing in front of her living room mirror. "Pure shit."

She pulls her full-length mink out of the closet—too heavy to walk long distances in, she wears it only for show; it's ancient now, and she sews it up with needle and thread like Sally Bowles when the skins dry and split—and ties the belt so that it's slung low around her hips, like a bathrobe. She plants her feet wide apart, and the bottom of the coat swirls around her in a whirlpool of fur at which she is the center. A modeling trick that she was taught to do in the nineteen-fifties, when men bought their women coats to show their love and to keep them happy: Hold your place, give the coat a shake so that it just grazes your shoulders, make it come alive.

We have a meal of memory and regret and heavy silence punctuated by the compulsive click of the silver Art Deco Tiffany compact I gave her on her birthday twenty years earlier, shortly after Ben's death, after we discovered that there was little left beyond the roof over her head.

I have stepped into the role of spouse and giver of gifts. This is sometimes self-serving, a form of protection: I want to make her happy, to dilute the indignation that bubbles inside her like a fountain, always triggered by the commonplace and trivial. The French sailor shirt I've grown fond of results in a night of her glaring at my stomach and offering me the name of a diet doctor *who used to work with Tarnower*. My horn-rimmed glasses instead of contact lenses. She stares at my head: a too-short haircut. Banality is the devil, and terrible enough to shove her over the edge of reason. Gifts are a momentary deflection.

Over dinner at a place where the food is consistent and the lighting kind, my mother is wistful and smiles sadly as she speaks of the past as if it were yesterday. Her recently highlighted blond hair, cut into an angular inverse Sassoon bob—the same long-in-front, short-in-back style she's been wearing since I was a child—is flawless. Beneath it, her kohl-lined eyes, rheumy and unfocused, betray her. Hers is a world seen through a web of dreams and time, a lamentation for what should have been the better life she deserved had the choices she made been different. Everyone got what they wanted, she says, except for her. The Talmudic dictum that she be *content with her portion* is elusive.

"Everyone deserves a good life, Mom," I tell her while we wait for the server to arrive. *"Everyone."*

"Not as much as me, darling," she says, flipping open her compact. "You don't even know."

She bites her lip and shuts her eyes and shakes her head. She begins The Telling; her work, her life, who she once was before I was born.

I let her speak without interruption. I order a glass of wine and then, a second. She stops talking and snaps to attention, as though she has been issued a small electric shock, more surprising than damaging. Her eyes dart from side to side.

"Women," she says, "don't drink like that."

"I do—" I say.

"It'll make you fat—"

"I'll risk it—" I say.

She puffs up her cheeks and like Marcel Marceau pantomimes a massively big belly, as if she were carrying twins.

Other diners eavesdrop and strain to hear her. They stare. The maître d'—a young gay man in stiff Selvedge jeans and a tight blue-and-white gingham shirt—fawns over her outfit: the Hermès purse, the baby-lotion-pink lace blouse opened nearly to her birdlike rib cage and exposing most of her left breast (*forgoddsake, nobody cares,* she says, when I motion to cover herself up)—the tight black leather agnès b. jacket bought on a whim one afternoon in SoHo in the eighties, when I was working across the street at Dean & DeLuca; Seaman Schepps shell earrings in a hazy apricot; an abundance of burly statement bracelets procured everywhere from the diamond district to the street vendors on Lexington Avenue.

My mother opens her purse and rummages through an old scuffed Vuitton makeup bag exploding with color, its zipper frayed and useless. She dumps out onto the table two different blushes, a massive wooden-handled brush, four silver metal tubes of lipstick, four eyeliner pencils whittled down to stubs like grade school crayons. She opens her silver compact again; she glances at it and draws dark brown circles around her eyes, over and over, until tiny dots of brown wax fleck her cheekbones. She clicks the compact closed and slides it back into its threadbare blue felt case and into her purse. One by one, the makeup items—the blush, the lipstick, the pencils, the brush—go back into the bag.

"What do you do?" the maître d' asks her. "You look so familiar."

"I am a performer," she says, with the faux-British lilt popular among nineteen-fifties movie starlets. She recounts her singing and modeling history as though it were yesterday. The radio shows. The silver loving cup she won on a local television competition when she was eleven. *My Oscar,* she calls it. The show on national television. The famous boyfriends. The Copa. The people who stop her in the street every day.

"And then," she says with a smile, "I had my daughter."

She nods across the table at me, past a litter of half-drunk lipstick-rimmed wineglasses of Sauvignon Blanc and the French wire basket of artisanal rolls vaguely picked over despite her recently acquired gluten allergy.

"This is your *daughter?*" the man says. "How nice to meet you."

I look up.

"Hard to believe, isn't it?" I roll my eyes and shrug. "I got all my father's genes."

The maître d' now has permission to laugh, and he does. I am my mother's court jester, her fool, the aggressively un-made-up, the plain to her striking, the wide to her narrow, the simple to her extraordinary. To be like her would have given her a fleeting moment of ease—the confirmation that I was merely an extension of her self, a younger reflection gazing back at her like Dorian Gray. It also would have been competition; it would have been too dangerous. We barely resemble each other and at least once during every meal at which I attempt to feed her—wherever we are: Balthazar, Starbucks, a diner—she pulls out a tube of her favorite Clinique lipstick in Red Red Red and thrusts it at me across the table. Desperate to please her, to keep the demons quiet, to give her a fleeting second of happiness be-cause it's my responsibility—*make me happy, just this once,* she begs; *do it for me, please make me happy*—I ask for her compact and swipe the bloody crimson across my lips. She stares. She smiles. She nods her head. She beams and claps her hands like a child.

"Yes," she coos—"Yes—look how *great* you look. Just *look* at you—"

I am wearing her face. She engulfs me.

I disappear.

. . .

THE TELLING IS ALWAYS THE same. She talks not to me but at me, her gaze yogic and soft, floating over my shoulder to the mirrored wall behind me. I let her go on this night at the bistro. I interrupt her; the server is clearing our plates.

"Do you want a cappuccino?"

"Am I dead?" she says. "I'm speaking."

"I just asked if you wanted a fucking cappuccino—"

"Forget it," she says, taking out her cell phone. "It's not important. And don't use that foul language. Who the *hell* taught you to speak that way?"

Years earlier, in her dimly lit Upper West Side office decorated with beige macramé wall hangings and antique Asian rugs, Anna, my therapist, would say, *The rules are different for dealing with an unquiet mind,* borrowing the words from Kay Redfield Jamison's memoir of mental illness and depression. *It's a pathology. It's not you. You have to remember that.*

She's never been diagnosed, I said. *She's just angry. She's always been this way.*

She's a walking DSM, my dear, Anna said.

I believe that Anna is wrong. I believe that it is me. I believe it is me when my mother rifles through my bag one day, finds a therapy bill, and calls Anna herself.

You're turning my daughter against me, Anna Haffner. I'll have you disbarred.

I apologize to my mother for the interruption; she has already forgotten it.

"You know, I was a very important singer—Jules Podell absolutely loved me. Everyone else, he terrorized—" she says of the Mafia-connected proprietor of the Copa, where she was a headliner and not, she makes sure I know, a Copa Girl "—but not me. Me, he *loved*."

I nod.

"I got home every morning at four and I had to be in the showroom at nine. I couldn't do it," she shrugs. "I was exhausted, so I quit modeling to sing. But your grandfather, he wouldn't pay for my lessons. Tight as a drum. Never even once came to see me on television. Wouldn't even *look* at me."

"I'm sorry—"

"He only loved *you*. *She has such smart eyes,* he used to say about you, and you were just a baby. You loved to make him laugh."

By the time she'd finished her run at the nightclub, my mother had been a model, a television singer with a string of demo records, and an on-again off-again relationship with the songwriter Bernie Wayne, author of "Here She Comes, Miss America" and a man twenty years her senior with an office in the Brill Building down the hall from Leiber and Stoller.

"We spent afternoons making out on his sofa," she says, sipping her coffee. "People were always coming in and dropping things off, and we didn't even look up."

When she and Bernie weren't together, she enraged him by showing up at the Stork Club on the arm of every eligible bachelor in New York and then in Cholly Knickerbocker's gossip column, where the boyfriend would read about it the next day. She talks obsessively about the clothes she wore, right down to the fabric and color—the Lanvin knockoffs, the Givenchy frocks—and the party that the television network threw for her at 21. The dress that her agent gave her right off her back— *Can you imagine,* she says, *I still have her business card sitting on the piano!*—in the ladies' lounge at Le Pavillon, moments before a press event.

Somewhere between the Stork Club and the frock and the time she left the Copa and had to step over Oscar Levant passed out in the gutter to get into a taxi back to her mother's house, she leans forward over what's left of the bread basket and the small chocolates that the server brought over on a small pewter tray and speaks to me directly; she breaks through the fourth wall. She sees me. She stops, as though a Pause button has been pressed. She focuses. She stares down at the table.

The coffee cup.

The chocolate wrappers.

Bread crumbs.

"Lissie, darling—" she whispers, reaching across the table for my hand.

"What, Ma—" I say, giving it to her. Her hands are so cold.

"I'm afraid—"

"So am I, Ma—"

When the bill for dinner arrives, I become the man: I palm over my credit card without looking at it, just as Ben would have done. I catch a glimpse of myself in the mirror behind my mother's banquette: my lip gloss chewed down to a hint of blush, my hair beginning to frizz from the humidity. I sign the receipt and gaze up to find her glaring at my eyes, her mahogany irises haloed by a tired sclera red-lined like a road map.

"Are you running out of makeup? Because a woman with no eyebrows is no woman at all."

I consider picking up the silver sugar dispenser—a coy little French contraption: a footed bowl with an attached lid on a hinge—and, because I don't throw like a girl, hurling it across the room, over the heads of the other diners sipping their wines and their Negronis, past the servers and the busing station, until it ricochets like a squash ball off a far wall of the restaurant behind the table where Tony Kushner is eating roast chicken.

"Your face is all red," she says. "Drop ten pounds. Even *five*—"

She shakes her head in dismay and we get up to leave, squeezing past the other tables and through the mirrored restaurant, down the street into her mirrored lobby where she pauses every few feet to check her face, into the mirrored elevator for the ride up to her mirrored apartment.

"But it was such a lovely dinner," I hear her say to someone on her bedroom phone, behind a closed door. "She always takes me for such lovely dinners."

. . .

WHEN MY MOTHER GOES TO bed, I busy myself the way I always do on my visits: I hunt for evidence of us, a trail of crumbs that will lead us to where we are now. I look for images of our past, proof of existence, glimmers of affection.

I unearth an ancient vinyl Alitalia travel bag from the den

closet. I rummage through thick stacks of peeling snapshots, fading SX 70 Polaroids, the Bruno of Hollywood medium-format professional portraits that mesmerized me as a child, not because of their empirical beauty but because I couldn't fathom that I was remotely related to her. Buried at the bottom of the Alitalia bag, curled in a letter C around a sheaf of my childhood postcards from camp in which I plead love for her in Cherokee pencil, my grade school report cards, and a few yellowing studio shots from her Copa days, is the picture of her sitting in front of my father's fake Pollock. The image of the woman who was once so glamorous she shimmered is literally wrapped around what she became: the dazzling, ambivalent mother to me: a plain child she never intended to have, the once-successful television star yearning only for what she once was and for what she might have become had her choices, made so long ago, been different.

"You don't even *know* what I gave up for you," she tells me in moments of rage. "You don't *even know.*"

I have stolen something from her, this stunning woman in the photo, the gold charm bracelet dangling off her wrist.

I have taken something from her—something vital and life-giving—and I have made it mine.

8

MY HIGH SCHOOL FRIEND TESS AND HER HUSBAND, PAUL, travel down from their home in Bangor to have dinner with us at our little rented cabin by the sea. Susan and I have spent the day close by, waiting for them to arrive. I have consulted my tide chart. We hike along the water's edge with Petey, who runs in and out of the waves, chasing seagulls and terns, barking furiously at surfers and kites and babies, and the spincasters who set themselves up for the day with a portable radio and a cooler filled with beer. I watch him, worriedly. Nature; acts of God. My fear: Something will catch his attention, the tide will turn, and he will be swept away.

————

Years ago, before I knew Susan and was still living in the city, I spent a week every July in Sconset, the farthest, wildest, most rose-covered edge of Nantucket. I was a guest of Sally, my best friend from college, her husband, William, and my friend's grandmother, a high-ranking member of an ancient European royal family toppled at the turn of the twentieth century. Maria, profoundly reserved and given to displays of neither wealth nor social register, rented annually a rambling gray cottage on a bluff overlooking the water. Our daily schedule was built around her; she took constitutional naps midmorning and in the late afternoon. We sat at the breakfast table together: coffee, eggs, ham, fruit, newspaper. Maria, dressed in older white slacks and a white cotton turtleneck, her lips swiped with a gloss of shimmering pearl pink lipstick, did the crossword puzzle and read the bridge column; William, the financial pages; Sally and I, everything else. We went to the beach and swam in the frigid water; we came home for lunch; we took late afternoon walks. At five o'clock every day, Maria woke from her second nap, changed for dinner, and, leaning against the butcher block kitchen island, drank two fingers of good bourbon; no more, no less. Maria's extended family from her second marriage, longtime summer residents of the island, came for lobster dinners eaten around a long table covered in flowered oilcloth; Maria sat at the head. Everything was planned and organized around her. She required nothing beyond peace and calm.

Life, she said—this woman who had, as a young girl, been imprisoned in a gulag, her family slaughtered—was hard enough. *Be in beauty; be with the people you love, who love you back, who require little more than kindness. Do the things that give you joy.*

In our early days together and even though it was just the two of us, Susan and I always rented big properties—rambling, drafty, nineteen-thirties lake cottages with creaking floors and room for ten. I imagined us waist-deep in the water, our shoulders burning under the hot August New England sun, teaching the young children in our family to swim and kayak. Cousins with babies would come; tiny bathing suits would dry on the line in the yard. A fire would be built; s'mores would be made. Blueberries would be picked and folded into a pie crust. They would spend two weeks with us, and every summer, they would look forward to it: Dates on calendars would be automatically blocked out, year after year.

My mother, I dreamed, would relax on a chaise, ensconced on the massive porch in a wide-brimmed straw hat, sipping iced tea, reading a fat novel and looking up from time to time, smiling. Content.

"Has she ever come?" Tess asks when I tell her my fantasy, and how our habit of beach cottage rentals first started: my visits to Nantucket, the belief that someday I could have the same, and that it somehow, miraculously, would replace the years of enmity, overtaking them like an eclipse. A do-over; a makeover.

"She's never been invited," I say.

Tess and I found each other on Facebook, where we are part of a core of old friends who knew one another in high school. People are very close; when a guy from my advanced placement English class develops pancreatic cancer, fundraisers are set up. When my friend Candy comes east from Santa Monica, parties are thrown and brunches given. Every Thanksgiving, a touch football game is organized in Flushing Meadow Park, in the shadow of our high school; college-aged children play alongside their fathers. Jokes are made about broken hips and knee replacements and walkers with tennis balls. There are divorces, illnesses, accidents, jobs lost, jobs found, aging parents. Kids are getting married; parents are dying. Who we are now is bound up with who we were then. I carry tucked into my wallet the Delmore Schwartz poem "Calmly We Walk Through This April Day." *Time is the school in which we learn / Time is the fire in which we burn.*

My friends post pictures of their children on a closed, private page. I post pictures of my mother. My friends knew her well; it was right after her divorce, and she fought with them, threw them out of our apartment, claimed that they stole from her, bummed Marlboro Lights off them, brought them along on my birthday to see *A Chorus Line.*

Wow, my friends write. *She's still so gorgeous.*

I've seen Tess three times in almost forty years, once right after college graduation, when she and her mother were traveling on the down escalator into the lobby of the World Trade Center and my father and I were traveling up to Windows on the World. We were both working our first jobs. She asked for my number and I gave it to her; I asked for hers and she said no.

We hadn't been close.

Tess left Forest Hills for good and after years of living in the city and working in advertising married a soft-spoken Mainer she'd met in college, an engineer. Active members of their local church, they recently moved from a solid, wide-porched bungalow built in the early nineteen hundreds—all foundation and solidity and weight—to a modern ranch house built of glass walls and angles and air. It's a curious thing when people do this—when they go from living in a home of one distinct style to another that is so utterly different, as though the form itself had become a bother, had grown tiresome and old, like fashion, or a hairstyle.

"It made sense," Tess told me, matter-of-factly. It would be easier for her elderly mother, who was still living in New York, to get around if she had to move in with them, which was looking like a distinct possibility.

"No stairs," she added.

On the day of their visit, we grill local cherrystone clams and mussels over a wood fire in a makeshift aluminum foil bag, tossing them hot with sweet butter, chopped garlic, and a handful of parsley in a blue ceramic bowl decorated with small lighthouses. We roast summer vegetables bought out of the back of a red Ford pickup parked on a state road in Lincolnville while we were driving back from the beach with the dog, who is covered in salt and sand. We open bottles of ice-cold white wine of middling quality; we drink to one another's good health, to our mothers, to time.

It's after dinner, and Susan is in the kitchen cleaning up; Paul is on the porch, playing my guitar. Tess and I sit opposite each other at the dining room table. Her hair, long and brown, to her shoulders, exactly how she wore it in high school, is beginning to gray. The contact lenses she started wearing in tenth grade have given way to thick glasses, a nearly undetectable line separating the top of the lenses from the bottom. She asks how I am.

"Fine," I say.

"No, really, she says. "How *are* you."

"I'm fine."

She's fine too, she says.

We're both fine. Everyone, we agree, is fine.

"How is everything with your mother," she says, leaning forward.

The universe that contains your mother. All that she encompasses; all that she swallows up, like Jonah and the whale.

"The way it's always been," I say. "Only now, she's older."

"So are you," Tess says, pushing her glasses up.

"So are *we*," I say.

"I brought you a gift," Tess says, folding her hands in front of her.

She unzips the small red-striped L.L.Bean boat bag on the chair next to her. She reaches in and extracts a tiny square hardback book covered with a bucolic out-of-register stock image of a flowering valley. Lush trees. In the distance, rolling hills. Tess reaches across the dinner table and hands me *Hope for Today,* published by Al-Anon Family Groups. The corner of a page is turned down.

I'm annoyed at the presumptuousness that this would even be remotely okay.

"You think I'm an alcoholic?" I say. "You don't even know me."

"I thought it could help with your mother," she says. "Read the page."

Please lead me to those who can give me what I need
and grant me the compassion to love those who can't.

9

AFTER SON OF SAM RAVAGED OUR QUEENS, NEW YORK, NEIGH-borhood, after the garbage strike of 1977 was over and his magazine business failed, my father and I spent his custody weekends floating through the city together in silence. We were a statistic, the midcentury detritus of divorce, and any-one looking at us—me makeupless, in Levi's, wide-striped rugby shirt, white-soled Topsiders, he in a boxy gray Harris tweed jacket and mossy green corduroys—would have as-sumed that we were on our way to pay a shiva call.

My arm linked tightly in his, our gait was loping and slow. We traversed the city in a trance: Central Park from Fifth Av-enue to Central Park West, Greenwich Village from Saint Mark's to Christopher, the Upper East Side from Madison to

First. Every weekend we retraced the previous one's steps, doing the things that my mother had taken little interest in during the sixteen years they were married.

Here were the carousel and the charcoal artists who set up their portable easels alongside the sailboat pond at Seventy-Second Street, and the statue of Alice in Wonderland, crawling with children. Here were the Eastern European restaurants, Vaselka and Christine's, and the building on East Ninth Street where my father's grandmother had lived until she died. Here was the Vanguard and Art Tatum and Chet Baker, the Met and the Guggenheim and the Whitney. Here was my father's unblinking fixation on Edward Hopper. *Early Sunday Morning*: a deserted city street, familiar, possibly New York, a strip of low-slung tenement buildings facing east, the sun glinting off three windows, their shades drawn, the ground floor storefronts obscured in darkness.

My father was making up for lost time, and these were activities that had their roots in exteriority and wonder; they demanded imagination. They took us outside ourselves and into a world at which neither my mother, nor we, were at the center. At the theater and the museum, my mother's spotlight would be eclipsed by a stranger, an artist she assured us didn't deserve it; at the Philharmonic, she got bored and fell asleep. Our days together in the city didn't orbit her past as a model and national television singer and what she was sure could have been, had her choices, made early on, been different. Art did not yield regret. My father and I went out in the world to see it, to absorb its possibility.

Every weekend, we sat for hours in the darkened MoMA

movie theater and watched Julie Christie in *The Go-Between*, and Fellini's *City of Women*. He loved the precision of Bach's cello suites, and we attended chamber music concerts in tiny jewel-box galleries that dotted the city. We watched the croquet players in Central Park, dressed from head to toe in crisp white outfits. We walked, we stopped, we sat side by side in silence eating damp Manhattan street pretzels like an elderly couple, bookends on splintering, green-painted park benches. We stopped for dinner at the restaurants of his bachelorhood; he drank dry gin Gibsons that made him cry for what he once had and lost, and he gave me a sip.

. . .

HE HAD BEEN A HANDSOME, blue-eyed Naval officer twelve years her senior, a dashing night fighter pilot flying off an aircraft carrier in the Pacific, a failed writer and poetry lover who returned to a career as a Madison Avenue advertising executive on a national butter campaign. She had been a professional singer from the age of three, first on radio and then on national television, an easily startled, blank-eyed only child born to stolid, older parents who reminded her every day of her life that she was fat and ugly and a mistake that they regretted. Her father, hunched over and his hair gone bone white in his twenties, a ringer for James Joyce given to neither public nor private displays of joy, admonished anyone who dared flatter his little girl, as though they might be lying to her.

My mother and I are sitting alone in her den a decade after I've left New York; I am visiting for the day from Connecticut. It is late in the afternoon, quiet and dusky, and we are drinking cups of tea. A new shipment of makeup from Saks has arrived, which will leave her little money for food for the month; the doorman thrust it into my arms on my way upstairs. More lipstick. More shopping. The space between stimulus and reaction; rather than fight with her, I try to understand. I ask her why. *Why. Why the piles of it in every room in her apartment.* She responds not with typical defense and rebuke. She tells me the story.

"I was with your grandfather at the candy store down the street from us in Brooklyn, and the man behind the counter said, *You have such lovely eyes, little girl—*"

"Well, you *do*—" I said.

She shook her head. *No—*

"Grandpa yelled at him. *Don't ever tell her that again,* he said to him."

I imagine my grandfather peering down at his daughter, round of face, her almond-shaped eyes the color of mahogany, swimming with tears. She was six, and standing at his elbow.

While she speaks, I gaze up at the studio shot of her hanging on the wall above her. She is in her twenties, lithe, willowy, swan-necked, with warm, empathic eyes that know. She had been told that she was ugly almost every day of her young life. She stored the words in her heart; pain became a universe that, as Claudia Rankine once wrote, was buried in her, that turned her flesh into its own cupboard.

"Mom—" I whisper. "He said that in front of you? Who says that in front of their child? I'm *sorry*—"

"*You're ugly,* he said, and I thought to myself, *Go to hell. I'll show you.*"

This child—this sad-eyed error, the result of a single, wedding night of combustion between two people who married because they were older and people were beginning to talk—starved herself to prove her father wrong. She really was beautiful and worthy of love; if not her parents', then everyone else's. She secretly sold her school lunch in order to stockpile makeup. Reapplying it obsessively at the first sign of its fading, she produced a different face, a mask. At Performing Arts High School, where she was one excellent young singer in a sea of talent, she lived on black coffee and cigarettes to lose the weight she was prone to; it tumbled off her. She morphed, before the world, into a stunning young woman who became a regular at the Stork Club and 21 and El Morocco. Life was her chess game: Every move she made was practiced and strategic as a guided missile. She would be beautiful and she would sing, and men, if not her own father, would worship her forever.

She was not pretty enough for her father; I was not pretty enough for my mother. A coil of grief rises into my throat and stops; I stand up from the couch and look out the window at the Upper West Side, the spires of the San Remo on Central Park West, and the park just beyond.

"More tea, Ma?"

She nods and I go into the kitchen and put the kettle on.

By the time my parents met in 1962, my mother had spent a season singing on national television; she was recognized on the street and regularly stopped for autographs. My father's well-off and formal family could find no fault with her. He had set eyes on her and had fallen in love; they married within months. After their first date, he took her back to her mother's apartment in a taxi for which he inadvertently didn't have enough cash to pay the fare. He was embarrassed; she was kind. The next day on his lunch break, he went to his family's jeweler on Forty-Seventh Street, bought her a tiny gold ring into which he stuck a rolled-up ten-dollar bill, and messengered it to the fur showroom where she was modeling, along with a note of profound apology.

"He was adorable and smart, but I should have known right then and there"—she told me years later, waving her index finger in the air—"he had a *little problem* with money."

A collision of hope and entitlement, hunger and expectation: My father wanted her to be the smiling trophy wife of his dreams, the sort of bombshell for whom he and thousands of men just like him had won the war. The prim heat of June Cleaver crossed with the smolder of Ann-Margret, hanging off his gabardine-suited arm as they careened around Kennedy's Manhattan, the world suddenly at their feet. He assumed that after a few years, they would move to the suburbs where they would live in a colonial with a deep backyard and produce a flock of children and grandchildren. There would be vacations and music lessons, a country club membership, a longtime career from which he would retire as senior vice president and creative director from his advertising agency with a company pension. Children were blips on my mother's radar; she lusted for the things that made her beautiful and desirable and that would stop time. My father longed for a sense of place, and we spent every weekend of my young childhood visiting the model

houses his company advertised, in communities called Levit-
town and Lake Success. I grasped their hands as we left my
father's Barracuda idling in recently paved driveways all over
Long Island and swung myself across the clear-plastic-carpeted
thresholds, feet in the air, like a small bride on her wedding
night.

But we would never leave Forest Hills; my father would
become a publisher and his business would go bankrupt. My
mother would turn her attention to men of greater success and
possibility.

I am all that remains of them. I look like my father, with his
sad, dropped brow and square build. I sound like him, and
when I cough I can feel his presence around me, although he's
been dead for sixteen years as I write this, longer than they
were married. I have his gait and his laugh, his smile, his temper, his humor, his tendency to melancholy. When my mother
asked him to leave, he remained a specter in her life, a ghost; I
so resembled him that I was a constant reminder of her ex-
husband in manner and countenance. Once he moved out, she
made herself scarce. She began to date Ben, her boss from the
fur showroom where she modeled and one of the most eligible
bachelors in the city. Every night, I was left in the care of Gaga,
a broad-boned, old-fashioned woman, white-blond, who had
shaken her fist at the *Hindenburg* as it sailed west to its doom
over her Brooklyn home in 1937. Gaga sat hour after hour in
our apartment while my mother was out with Ben at Studio 54
and Plato's Retreat. I adored her; she fed me a simple dinner,

returned to her chair, and waited for her daughter to return home.

My sleep was fitful and I stumbled into the pitch-black living room at two in the morning to find her sitting there, eyes closed, chin on her chest.

"Where is she, Gaga?" I whispered, touching her arm.

"Your mother forgot to come home, Elissala. Go back to bed."

. . .

ON A SATURDAY AFTERNOON NOT long after the divorce, my father took me for lunch to the sort of place my mother would have refused to set foot in; she would have waited for us in the car. He fetishized it as slumming—*it'll be fun,* he said. We sat side by side at the lunch counter at Brennan and Carr, a sliver of a restaurant in deepest Brooklyn, surrounded by cops and firemen on break, hunched over tiny jus-soaked roast beef sandwiches that dripped down our chins. Someone mopped the floor with Ajax while we were eating. The doors to the place were flung open and the stench of the city permeated everything like acid through plastic: meat and steam and ammonia and garbage and hot concrete.

"I want you to remember," he said. "Someday, she'll be your responsibility." He wiped his face with a napkin. "You'll never be able to give her what she wants. I tried. But someday, she will be your job."

We had been eating in silence; he had been thinking about it. We were a newly divorced family. She was not yet married to Ben. My father would not meet Shirley, his second wife, a professor of psychology at Brooklyn College with a thriving private practice specializing in the treatment of trauma victims and survivors of war, for another four years. I was making a list of colleges, all of them far away: Colorado, Berkeley, Stanford. I didn't discuss my plans with my mother and she never asked.

Was my father predicting the inevitable? Did he foretell a future in which her money would drip dry, the open spigot of need destroying her from the inside out, the desperate hunger for a past in the spotlight clinging to her ankles like a street urchin? Could he know that someday, forty years into the future, I would be faced with a decision based on moral obligation, primal devotion, and the vain hope for redemption and resolution: to rescue her, to find a way for us to heal.

"The Fifth Commandment," my father said that afternoon. "Honor thy mother and father. No matter what."

10

THE DISPATCHER DOESN'T CALL IN THE ACCIDENT AS AN EMER-
gency, and it takes half an hour for the ambulance to arrive.
She isn't having a heart attack or a stroke. She hasn't fallen
in the street. There is no blood. She's conscious. My mother
is sitting on the floor near the front door to her Upper West
Side apartment, one foot twisted grotesquely out of joint. A
bit of light brown bone nudges through the taut, papery skin.
The other foot, the good one, is slowly swelling from a metatarsal fracture.

She had spent the day walking. She stood, she said, and
that's all she did: Both feet were asleep. They caught, tangled,
and twisted when she got up from the couch where she was
watching Joan Fontaine in *Rebecca*.

———

It's nearly Christmas. The performers' club where she sings
every week is having their holiday party. A few years earlier,
Abe Vigoda had begged her to be his date.

Please, Rita darling, please, said the familiar deep voice on
her answering machine while I stood there listening to the leg-
end ask my mother out. She shook her head at the phone, eyes
clenched tight with dramatic regret as though Abe himself
could see her through the wires.

"Absolutely *not*," she moaned to me. "They'll all think I'm
ninety."

But on this night, being at the club for the Christmas party
is all she can think about.

"I wanted to go so bad," she wails loud enough for the dispatcher to hear her. "I wanted to sing tonight—I *must* sing. I
was practicing 'I'll Be Home for Christmas'—"

"Is she having trouble breathing?" the dispatcher asks me.

"She passed out twice while we were on the phone with
her," I say.

"Don't you lie to them!" she yells from the living room.
"You'll *lie* to them! I can hear you from here!"

"Is she abnormally agitated, Ma'am?"

"Not abnormally, no—"

"And her breathing is okay?"

"It is."

"Chest pains?"

"No chest pains."

My mother, fully made up from her day, is the color of a
bleached bedsheet. When I hang up with the dispatcher, the
signs of shock come back to me in a vague rush from my Red

Cross training days when I was the teenage lifeguard my father said would never drown because of my outsized breasts.

"Ma, are you nauseous?"

She shakes her head no.

"I didn't eat anything," she says. "Maybe there's a cookie?"

"Are you cold?"

She shakes her head no.

"Am I gonna need a operation? Because I don't want a operation—"

Her voice is high and reedy. Her words come out unadorned, her grammar mangled. A slip of a moment: I want to take her in my arms, like an injured child. My stomach falls. I can't.

"We don't know yet," I say, bending down to her. I put my hand on her knee and she stares at it. It feels alien, disembodied. I remove it.

"—and I can't have a operation because I'm allergic—"

Which is true: Since I was a small child, she has suffered from allergies to the world around her. One huge allergy, unwieldy as a tuba, to everything from the dyes used in soap and shampoo and every brand of makeup except for Clinique, to the elemental and natural: dirt and sun.

"Just give me an ice pack," she says. "No surgery."

I position the living room table lamp above her so that it's shining on her without her knowing. I look at her pupils.

Years earlier, when I was a camp counselor in the early nineteen-eighties, I was in charge of ten eight-year-olds for two months, and one of my girls suffered a compound fracture of her wrist while playing kickball. In the middle of a grassy field, mosquitoes humming around us, she shook in my arms. I asked about her puppy. We waited for the ambulance to arrive. She shivered; I held her. She went into shock. Her eyes went black. My mother, at eighty-two, her foot dislocated nearly behind her, was deciding whether to take a painkiller.

"Gimme a Tylenol," she says to Susan, who goes into the kitchen and comes back with two capsules.

"Just *one*," my mother says, holding up her index finger.

"Take two," Susan says, bending down to give her the pills with a glass of water.

"*One—*"

"*Two—*"

My mother screws up her face.

"Not the *pink* one," she says, shoving Susan's hand away. "I can't take the pink one. You should remember that. Get me a tablet. *White.*"

"Rita, the capsule will get into your system faster," Susan says.

"*I. Am. Allergic. To. The. Color. Pink.* What is *wrong* with you?"

Susan goes back into the kitchen to get her the single Tylenol—plain; white—which will do for her injury as much as a sugar pill, and is the only thing my mother will take for the pain that she is not entirely sure she feels.

It takes thirty minutes for the ambulance to arrive. Wanda the EMT, built like a small refrigerator, is all business, no bullshit, and trained not to appear shocked. We learn on the way to the hospital that she is an Iraq War veteran, a medic. She has seen her friends explode like water balloons after driving over IEDs. Wanda looks at my mother's ankle and gasps.

"How much discomfort are you in, Ma'am?"

My mother shrugs.

"A little."

"What did you take for the pain?"

"A Tylenol. The white one. I'm allergic to the pink one. I swell up like a fat cow."

She puffs up her cheeks and pats her belly.

"Do you have anything stronger? Percocet?"

My mother straightens up. Her eyes bulge. She winds up like a pitcher.

"Why the *hell* would I have that? Are you *accusing* me?"

She glares at me. She wags her index finger so furiously that I'm certain it will snap off and cartwheel end over end across the living room to the piano, where it will land in the silver loving cup she won for a singing competition in Brooklyn when she was thirteen, right after the war was over.

"Did my daughter tell you I'm a druggie? *Did she*? Her father—now *he* was the hypochondriac. He'd take anything he could get his hands on."

"For Chrissakes, Mom—"

"Don't you start with *me*—"

"A lot of people have it in their house," Wanda says to her. "Dental work, surgery—"

"I will not take anything more than a Tylenol white," she says, folding her arms across her chest. "I am not like her father, the bastard. *He* was the hypochondriac. Not me—"

Wanda pulls me into the kitchen while her partner settles my mother onto the stretcher and straps her in.

"Tough old bird. Dementia?"

"No—" I say.

"You sure? Agitation comes with dementia. Maybe a UTI?"

"She was born like this," I tell her.

"Anything else? Cancer? Mental illness?"

"No—"

Wanda stares at me over her glasses.

"This is her normal," I say. "This is who she is—"

"Really?"

"Really—"

"Because this much agitation can take a physical toll if it goes on for a long time."

"Forever—" I say.

"Falls?" Wanda asks.

"Two years ago."

"What happened?"

"We were in San Francisco over Christmas. We got a call on New Year's Eve morning from the emergency room at Mount Sinai."

"Hip?"

"Dehydration. She fell through the plastic shower door in her bathroom and scraped up her face. She hadn't eaten in days."

We had raced home from the West Coast. I drove to her apartment as soon as I could get there. She greeted me at the door in full makeup—thick pink swipes of blush, heavy chocolate-brown eyeliner, black mascara, Red Red Red Clinique lipstick—her face bruised, her eyes nearly swollen shut like George Foreman's after a round in the ring. She'd refused lidocaine for the stitching.

"Why didn't you bite on a fucking bullet, Ma? It's not the movies, forgoddsake."

"Allergic—and anyway I didn't feel anything," she shrugged, holding an ice pack to her cheek.

"St. Luke's," Wanda says to her partner, walking back into the living room.

"New York Hospital," my mother says, cutting her off. "I'm only going to the Upper East Side."

"We need to get you to the closest one," Wanda says.

"New York. East Sixtieth or I'm not going anywhere."

"But—"

"My kid was born there," she says, looking over at me. "So that's where we're going, or I'll scream." She folds her arms across her chest. She's the decider.

We collect her things: wallet, handbag, makeup case.

In the ambulance, the second EMT takes more vitals: blood pressure, pulse, blood oxygen level. Unremarkable.

"Who's president?" he says.

"That animal. I made his first wife a fur coat."

"How old are you?"

"Sixty."

The EMT stares at me.

"But you have Medicare," he says.

"They made an exception for me," she says.

I stand at the nurse's station outside her room in the emergency department on a late Saturday night. Gurneys charge past us. Gunshot wounds. A stabbing. A meth overdose. Two heavily armed police officers flank the triage area. A priest races down the hallway, his black loafers squeaking on the linoleum. The smell of blood and shit and ammonia fill the stagnant air.

"We'll need her papers," the nurse tells me. "Living will, healthcare proxy, any other directives. Do you know her wishes?"

"No idea," I say.

"She never told you?" the nurse asks, looking up from her computer screen.

"Not a clue."

Years earlier, Susan and I had our papers drawn up. *Susan is my healthcare proxy,* I told my mother, hoping that acknowledging my own mortality would compel her to acknowledge hers. *Shouldn't you have one too?* I asked.

You're trying to kill me, she screamed. *You'll have a bad day and shut me off, just like you did your father. Flip a switch.*

He was brain-dead, Mom—

That's not my problem.

So, no papers.

"Are there any other children?" the nurse asks. "Grandchildren?"

"No other children. No grandchildren. My wife and I have no children."

The words catch in my throat like a fish bone. My eyes burn from the ammonia in the air.

"A husband? She's wearing a wedding ring."

"It's her mother's," I say.

Susan and I have been awake for thirty hours, sixteen of which have been spent sitting in folding chairs alongside my mother's stretcher, while they pump her full of Demerol. She fights them; they threaten restraints; she screams. My chest aches when I look at her. I want to run, to take Susan by the hand and flee down the hallway, out to York Avenue, back to our car, back to Connecticut. I want to run, to stay, to reach out and hold her hand, to comfort her. It feels alien, like tearing through a membrane.

"They won't touch her until she signs a directive," the nurse says. "Her age. Hospital liability."

She has never discussed her plans with me. I have no idea what she does or doesn't want. Whether she would sign a DNR or even where she wants to be buried. There is no cemetery plot. Cemeteries repel and repulse her; she has never visited her parents, since her mother died in 1982. When I begged her to draw up the most basic of healthcare proxies after my father died in a car accident, she found an entertainment lawyer in the Yellow Pages who charged her four hundred dollars for his time, printed the papers off the internet, and never had them notarized. But he promised to make her a star.

"He'll *do* things for me," she warned "—so don't you mix in and screw it up."

I call our lawyer in Connecticut on Sunday morning, the day after the accident. In three hours we have a directive in hand, along with a new healthcare proxy. My mother agrees to sign both of them in front of the hospital notary public.

"You are not allowed to speak during this process," he says to me.

He turns to my mother.

"In your own words, do you want to be resuscitated?"

"Are you *crazy*? Of course I do! Over and over and over again. That's a *ridiculous* question. Are you one of those people who think everyone over sixty should be allowed to die?"

"Do you want a feeding tube if one is necessary, Ma'am?"

"A *what?*"

"A feeding tube," he says.

"Up my nose?"

"Down your throat, to provide you with nutrients. With food—"

"Absolutely *not,*" she says. "I'll eat when I'm hungry. I don't need anyone feeding me."

The notary looks at me. I can't speak.

"Do you understand that you're saying you want to be resuscitated but that you don't want the nourishment needed to keep you alive? You may be unconscious—"

"I understand exactly what I'm saying," she says. "No food unless I ask for it. I *refuse* to get fat."

We sit in a crowded, musty waiting room filled to capacity. An extended family—siblings and friends and neighbors, a young man in gang colors—gather around the mother of a stabbing victim, who is being interviewed by a police officer. A group of Orthodox Jewish men, black-hatted and ancient-eyed, pray quietly near an eastern-facing window for an elder undergoing heart surgery. A tired Hispanic woman, her eyes red and swollen from crying, sits by herself. An old friend, an infectious disease nurse who works at the hospital, comes by during a break from her shift and waits with us.

The act of waiting is not a sentimental one; to see people, related by blood or not, sitting quietly in a badly furnished, airless room, its noise level artificially flattened by the din of wall-mounted televisions tuned to the banal and the ridiculous, is to come face-to-face with the tribal. We don't sit with people and wait for the tumor to be excised or the heart to be repaired or the incision to be stitched. We sit and wait as evidence of life and circle, as a way to peer together over the edge of possibility and time. We sit and wait because the human condition is not to be alone; not to be abandoned.

A ten-hour surgery to reconstruct my mother's ankle with an articulated plate and seventy-five titanium screws secured to spongy osteoporotic bone.

At hour four, I have a massive spontaneous nosebleed that leaves me woozy and my heart racing. Susan cleans me up, holds my hand, tilts my head back.

I am called by the recovery room nurse.

"She's awake," she says, "but she's very groggy. You can stay for five minutes."

I imagine it this way:

I will creep in and hold her hand. I will kiss her forehead. She will whisper I love you, Lissie. I will whisper back I love you too, Mom. I always have.

Dark mascara streaks run down the sides of her face into her ears. Evidence of the lipstick they wiped off before they intubated her is smeared across one cheek.

"I'm so sorry for everything," she says in a hoarse voice, barely recognizable.

"I'm sorry too, Mom," I say, rubbing her hand. "I love you. I'm so sorry—"

Tears that will not stop.

I rest my head on the side of her bed. She rakes her fingers through my hair.

"Lissie darling—get your highlights—"

"I love you so much, Mom."

I am led down the hallway by the surgical waiting room manager. My mother is in the first bed with a dedicated post-op nurse named Svetlana, who is monitoring her vitals.

There is giggling. I stand at the foot of my mother's bed. She is flat on her back, her feet elevated in huge plastic cam boots. She and Svetlana are laughing.

"I told her to Google me up, honey," my mother slurs, lifting her head. She waves at me with a limp hand, her pupils wide as black marbles.

Svetlana spins my mother's monitor around so that I can see her blood pressure, blood oxygen level, pulse. She wants me to see how well my mother is doing, after such a hideous accident and the violent daylong surgery required to save her.

There on the screen is my mother on a recent fashion website, dressed in an orange sheared mink shrug thrown over a silk blouse the color of bone, with her massive round signature glasses and bright red lipstick. She poses for the camera on her terrace, unsmiling and cool, nostrils flared, chin tipped up, hand on her hip. She floats twenty-one stories above the Upper West Side, the rest of Manhattan behind her in the distance, everyone walking and walking, all of them a blur.

11

HER RIGHT KNEE IS BENT INWARD TOWARD HER LEFT, HER LEFT foot pointed away from its mate, its tender and narrow ankle sharply rolled under and on to the ball of her foot, to near disjoint. The intended effect: a slimming of the leg, a prim taunt, a come-hither beckoning.

In 1980, with the ink not yet dry on her divorce papers, my mother takes up tennis. Ben, whom she will marry in a year, belongs to a Westchester country club on a narrow country road anchored from end to end with yellow clapboard farmhouses. She wants me to teach her how to play. I'm suspicious. My mother hates sports. She has no eye-hand coordination. She hates to sweat. She owns no sneakers, no shorts, no polo shirts, no sweat socks, no T-shirts. She's never swung a tennis racquet before in her life.

Teaching her how to play tennis feels like a ploy, a mercenary setup.

"Are you fucking kidding me?" I say. "Why?"

She has barged into my bedroom, dressed for the day in a jewel-toned jacquard Missoni sweater and loose raw linen trousers the color of wheat. She fingers my grandmother's massive jade beads, which she has recently begun wearing like a talisman: green, she says, is the color of money.

I am sixteen. A pair of stereo headphones hangs around my neck like a choker. I roll my eyes, I laugh at her. Her face turns red. I snicker. I'm wary and I'm cruel and I want nothing to do with her. *The Eagles' Greatest Hits* is on my turntable. *I found out a long time ago what a woman can do to your soul.*

"Because I asked you—that's why," she says through clenched teeth. "Because I am your mother. *I. Am. Your. Mother.* I demand that you teach me."

Fuck, I mumble under my breath. *Fuck it.*

"Can't you just ask the pro?"

Nick is twenty, Bain de Soleil–tanned, with a mane of shaggy blond hair that makes him look like a cross between Bjorn Borg and a golden retriever. Every day at one, when the sun is at its highest point in the sky, he pulls his shirt off and plays in only his tennis shoes, socks, and tiny white shorts, a tuft of golden man fur sprouting deep from the cavern of his back. He loves the ladies and they love him. Mrs. Stone, whose husband is in drapery, has a seasonal room at the club, and Nick delivers her dinner himself every night while Mr. Stone stays back in the city. Why, I want to know, can't my mother ask Nick.

"Because I want *you*—" my mother says, pointing down at me like Uncle Sam.

The tennis court is my territory, a planet in the universe I've constructed for myself where I keep the rest of the world at bay. While my high school friends are blowing their boyfriends in the back of bright orange Firebirds parked in abandoned lots all over Queens, I spend every afternoon in a nearby middle school playground pounding a fucking ball against a fucking wall for hours before dinner. Eventually, I play competitively— there will be camps and teams and closets stuffed with racquets and crates of balls—and our living room will be covered with plaques that hang from the wall and trophies that stand on the piano next to my mother's loving cup. Tennis belongs to me. She wants what is mine.

"So can I borrow your shorts?" she says. "I'd ask Ellen, but she's too fat."

"Ellen's a six, Mom—"

Our next-door neighbor is tiny, an Auschwitz survivor who, tormented with grief and guilt, stopped eating once the war was over.

"I want yours. The pleated ones."

"You hate pleats."

"GIVE ME YOUR SHORTS OR I WILL *KILL* MY-SELF!"

She balls up her fists and fake-beats them on the sides of her head. The dog, who has been asleep on my bed, runs into the living room, his tail between his legs.

I grew up in a home where the threat of suicide was tossed over one's shoulder like grains of salt. *Put on more lipstick or I'll kill myself,* my mother shrieked every morning when I left our apartment for middle school, and every afternoon, I stopped on the street, halfway home, and reapplied my Bonne Bell Lipsmacker, terrified that I'd open our door and there she'd be, stretched out on the plastic-covered love seat like Jacques-Louis David's painting of Marat dead in his bathtub.

My diary for this day, written in runny blue Bic pen in a gray lab notebook plastered with Mirabai Bush rainbows and daisies:

Mom. Suicide. Shorts.

"Take them," I say, pulling a pair out of my dresser drawer. She storms out and slams the door. Paint crackles off the frame and onto the floor.

Five minutes later, she is back.

"So what do you think?" she asks.

She poses in front of my mirror, left foot out, ankle down, hands on her hips. A hair toss, and she grabs an inch of loose material from beneath her navel and grimaces. She turns to the side, looks over her shoulder, sucks in her cheeks.

"I can safety-pin the waist. When did you get so big?"

She leaves in a blur.

I lock the door, strip my T-shirt and bra off, and stare into my full-length mirror, dressed from the waist down in worn Levi's and navy blue Pro Keds.

I put my hand on the tiny mark under my left breast, at the top of my rib cage. I close my eyes.

. . .

ON A LATE SATURDAY MORNING between the end of summer and the start of my senior year in high school, I travel by subway from our apartment to Grand Central Station. I ride Metro-North up to the Mount Kisco stop in northern Westchester, where a local taxi picks me up and takes me, my tennis clothes, and a bag of racquets and balls up to the Valley Club, where my mother has arrived with Ben a day earlier. By noon, mother and daughter stand face-to-face on the dusty green Har-Tru tennis court. I am on one side of the net in my white Izod polo shirt and red nylon gym shorts. My mother stands on the other side in a tight white sequined Studio 54 T-shirt, full makeup, and jewelry: a few massive turquoise and silver pieces from Mexico, her broken mood ring, the little round monogrammed gold charm that I bought for her birthday, massive gold hoop earrings, my grandmother's jade. My pleated white Fred Perry shorts hang away from her narrow legs like a potato sack. She wears white leather Capezio ballet flats with nude nylon peds. She does not intend to run.

"Shake hands with the racquet, Ma," I say. "Make friends with it."

She holds it loosely in an eastern grip, the racquet head at eye level.

"Take it back the minute the ball crosses the net. Okay? And keep your eye on the ball."

She nods. She walks back to the T. She gives her Toni Tennille bowl haircut a toss and straightens her spine. She holds the racquet up the way I told her to.

"*Ready,*" I call out through megaphone hands.

My mother tucks an errant strand of mahogany hair behind her ear, rests the racquet on her shoulder the way they do in *Town and Country,* and poses as though she's in the show-room: right knee in toward her left, left foot pointing away toward the next court, left ankle parallel to the ground, her instep almost brushing the court.

A few of the club's members—tidy Westchester ladies wearing gold add-a-bead necklaces and Lilly Pulitzer tennis dresses and carrying wooden-handled, monogrammed Ber-muda bags—are gathered around by the chain-link fence.

"Ready . . . hold your racquet the way I said—"

She nods again, fiddles with her hair. She looks around her. She knows she's being watched. She holds her head up, rests the racquet on her shoulder, and poses. The ball sails over the net and past her to the fence.

"Let's try again . . . Can you at least swing?"

She nods. She fiddles with her hair. She looks around and sighs. She's bored and distracted. She poses. I lob another ball across the net. It sails past her and jangles off the fence.

"Can you leave your hair alone?"

She drops the racquet and walks to the net.

"There is *no reason* not to look good," she says through clenched teeth.

The club ladies think that mother and daughter are up at the net discussing grips and strokes and swings and whether a two-handed backhand is more effective than the traditional version. I squint up at her head, which is blocking the rays of the sun like an eclipse.

"You're not in the showroom, forgoddsake," I say. "Why did you even bring me here?"

"Don't you *dare* talk to me that way," she growls. "You're just trying to make me look bad because you don't like Ben. You want me to be alone. *I know why you're doing this*—I'm send-ing you home."

"Don't send me," I say, starting to walk off the court. "I'm leaving."

"If you leave, I'll change the locks. I'll throw your things out."

"I'll go to Gaga's."

"She won't let you in either."

Silence.

We glare at each other, panting and snorting like hot, angry animals: me, the tomboy daughter she never expected to have, the one she had no idea what to do with, the one who was not her mirror image. She, the bombshell mother, full of beauty and longing and regret. A showdown on a tennis court in the middle of Westchester on a sunny Saturday afternoon. The O.K. Corral with Tab and grosgrain headbands.

She threatens me with banishment: She will turn me away, set me loose in the desert to wander, the Torah's sacrifice—the Azazel, the scapegoat. *I will throw you out and my life will go on.* I imagine stepping off the elevator, turning right down the hall-way toward our apartment, and all of my things—my suitcases, guitars, mandolins, tennis racquets, albums, stereo, books—piled up outside the door, like the Joads right before Tom straps everything to the Ford. The piano, bought for me by Gaga and taken over as a piece of living room furniture, stays behind.

I imagine going across the street to Gaga's. I ring the doorbell.

"Go away," Gaga says through the tiny metal peephole above the doorbell. "We don't want you anymore."

Because of tennis. Because my mother didn't swing her racquet.

On this day at Ben's Westchester country club, tucked quietly down a leafy road off Route 22, I have been lured into the role of foil; I am ever, always hopeful that by giving her what she wants, what she needs—Who might the mark on my rib have become?—she will be happy and safe, the desperation will dissipate and slow, and we will be re-formed, and our relationship made fresh and new.

This time will be different; we will be healed.

My mother has as much interest in playing tennis as in performing brain surgery. This is a performance, a recital of sorts, meant not for us but for the other club women—the Bermuda bag ladies who have standing weekend games with their coltish teenage private school daughters with names like Bitsy and Muffy—to see us together on the court, Brenda Potemkin and her doting mother, wealthy, loving, inseparable. An affectionate daughter teaching her adoring mother how to play the game of the rich and well-heeled, the assimilated and American. A mother genuinely interested in her only child's favorite activity. If I don't play the role she has assigned me, I will fail her.

I look up to see Ben waiting outside the court. He is a nice man from Pennsylvania, all tie and loafers and old-fashioned manners. Beyond being, as my mother likes to call him, The Most Important Furrier in the City of New York, Ben's claim to fame is that his cousin, a well-known Los Angeles animator, was the creator of Mr. Magoo, modeling the bumbling, half-blind character after him.

He looks really familiar, my friends say when they meet him, *but I can't place him.*

It is impossible for me to dislike him.

Ben waves me over while my mother is sitting on the court bench fiddling with her purse, pulling open her Vuitton makeup case, rummaging around for her lipstick.

"I don't know what it is with you two," he says. "Stay, please. We'll have a nice lunch. She's just frustrated."

"About what?" I ask. "That she had to hit a ball? Why did she even want me here?"

"Just stay," he sighed. "Please—we'll have a nice lunch."

We sit together in the country club's pub room in silence. She stares at my hair. Ben stares at the television. Hot dogs turn on a rotating grill behind the bar, sending up clouds of gamy porcine grease into the air. Ben orders a beer and a burger. I want a beer and a burger. My father, when we spend our weekends together, always lets me order alcohol: wine, beer, Slivovitz when it's freezing, cognac when it's not. We joke that I have a hollow leg; my capacity for a good lager, chilled down in an ice-rimed pitcher, is boundless.

"She'll have a small salad and a Tab," my mother instructs the waiter, nodding over at me. "I'll have a bagel, scooped out, fat-free cream cheese on the side."

She never sets foot on a tennis court again.

"She just doesn't want me to play," my mother stage-whispers to a woman in the locker room while I change out of my whites a few feet away. "I embarrass her," she says.

"They're all embarrassed at seventeen," the woman says.

That morning at the club—just like every morning: at the school bus stop, on the subway platform, putting makeup on in the bathroom—my mother posed hard and jutting, her legs at a sharp angle, her left foot leaning on its arch, bent out of shape. Her ankle is a fulcrum for her beauty; it bears the weight of vanity and loveliness and time.

"I stood up," she told Svetlana in the hospital recovery room after her surgery, "and it was asleep."

She rolled it, and after so many years of pressure and stress, it snapped.

12

IN 1985, I RETURNED TO NEW YORK CITY AFTER GRADUATING from college in Boston and lived with my mother and Ben in his boxy white-and-Lucite-festooned postwar high-rise apartment on the Upper West Side. When the weather grew chilly, Ben and I left her at home in bed watching old movies and went shopping together so that I could cook him the rich, comforting dishes of his Pennsylvania childhood: goulashes and stews and briskets and roasts. He double-parked their Volvo sedan in front of Fairway while I went from aisle to aisle with other women ten years my senior, new mothers pushing metal carts overflowing with food, sleeping infants strapped to their chests in colorful Snuglis. Hours later, lured by the smell of caramelizing onions or crushed tomatoes cooked down to a garlicky jam, my mother emerged from their bedroom while I stood at her stove, wooden spoon in hand, wrapped in a ruffle-edged Playboy apron left behind by Ben's last girlfriend.

"I *know* you know how to cook," my mother whispered in my ear one cold afternoon. "You don't have to be so obvious about it."

Pictures taken at the time show me unsmiling and glassy-eyed and looking vaguely as if I'd swallowed a handful of Quaaludes, dressed in clothes that I allowed my mother to select for me because it seemed only right and gave her such pleasure: I was living under her roof rent free and making a salary that made independent life in nineteen-eighties Manhattan impossible. She dressed me as herself: Gorgeous four-inch brown suede Italian pumps that I walked in as though they were stilts. A gold brocade double-breasted custom-tailored suit that looked like curtains torn from the windows of a Borscht Belt hotel dining room. The two-sizes-too-small silk blouses that she brought home from Lucille, who still worked in the garment center.

With tits like yours, it pays to advertise, she'd say, unbuttoning them as low as she could while I stood with my hands at my sides, like a mannequin.

Together, we played house; their friends became my friends. At twenty-two, I was married to them, an appendage meant to dress, look, and act like a scaled-down version of my mother, tacking down the seams of our life as they frayed. On Super Bowl Sundays, I mixed up Tiffany crystal pitchers of stiff Bloody Marys, to Ben's friends' delight and shouts of *You're hired!* and *You shoulda married her!* Holiday meals were spent dining around tables for ten in the Pool Room at the Four Seasons and Mr. Chow. Ben's friends, men thirty and forty years older than I, some dining with the longtime mistresses I assumed were their wives, slipped me their private office numbers under the table while their women rolled up delicate slices of lemon chicken in lettuce leaves and talked about their hairdressers, who were all, suddenly, dying.

"Animals—you can't even use their fucking toilets anymore," Ben's friend Harry Stein said. He ran his hand up my leg under the table while shoveling Day-Glo sweet and sour chicken into his mouth. Grains of rice clung to his lips; his belly popped open the middle button on his black silk shirt. He leaned forward, mouth wide, barking like a pit bull, one hand waving his fork in the air, the other under the table up to his elbow, groping around for my crotch.

"Bernice," I said to Harry's hair-sprayed wife, "tell your husband to get his fucking hand off my thigh," and he did, and we all howled with laughter.

Side by side, we rose in the mornings, drank our Mr. Coffee black and sweet, and went off to work—my mother and Ben to their downtown fur salon where she spent her days modeling sable and mink for the wives of O.J. Simpson and Willie Nelson, me to my desk job as a publishing assistant—and afterward met for dinner with their friends at an old-school steak house famous for its piano bar. While my colleagues were snorting coke in the bathroom at Canastel's and the Limelight, Ben and I sipped the first of our drinks and someone handed my mother a Shure 58 microphone and she snaked the cord through her left hand, performance style, and belted out show tunes with a voice so loud that the restaurant's artwork rattled against the wall.

Head thrown back, eyes closed, brow furrowed, heavy makeup dewy under the hot halogen lights, my mother was transformed into a woman from another time and place, who once stood on a soundstage on live television for two purposes: to look beautiful and to sing. Every night after work, we went out and my mother sang and sang, song after song, surrounded by Ben and me and a throng of middle-aged men, gazing at her like a pack of drooling jackals while their wives and mistresses stood around snickering. Ben's friends wanted to steal her from him, to woo her away, to give her whatever she wanted. Their wives wanted to strangle her. Her accompanists wanted to be her. Every night after work I watched my mother through a slosh of cold white wine, bursting with the same sort of chaotic pride that one has for a gifted young child playing a piano recital.

I'm related to her, the pride says. *That child with the microphone is mine.*

. . .

I LIVED IN HER APARTMENT for two years, amid the Lucite and the Baccarat, the nightly performances and the weekend Bloody Marys, until a series of ruptured ocular vessels began to

regularly flood my eyes with blood, and my doctor made moving out a medical necessity.

"You'll have a stroke by the time you're twenty-five if you
stay," he said.

When I finally left, I moved into a fifth-floor walk-up apartment in a seedy section of the city that I knew she'd never visit.
She wouldn't climb the stairs; she wouldn't step over the va-
grant living in the vestibule with his spent crack vials. She
hated my roommate and the piles of smoky quartz crystals and
incense holders and *Creative Visualization* tapes that Julie
brought to the apartment with her.

"Come over and have brunch with us," I said, inviting my
mother to visit shortly after I moved in. I had set up my first
kitchen with my father's help, and we filled it with heavy French
copper pots, a long butcher block island on wheels, a wall of
cookbooks, and small Duralex glasses out of which one might
drink wine or eat chocolate *pots de crème*. I wanted to cook for
my mother in my own home, as though the act of feeding and
nurturing her would unravel our rage like a kinked phone cord.

"I don't need to see *that girl*," my mother snarled. "There's
something about her I just don't like. But you can come here.
I'll order a chicken. I have a little surprise for you—"

That Saturday afternoon, I crossed Central Park and arrived at my mother's before noon. She opened the door and
there she stood, smiling broadly, dressed in an outfit identical
to what had become my late-eighties uniform, which I had
worn practically every day since moving out of her apartment:
narrow khakis, a white Gap T-shirt, a strand of fake pearls, a
stack of black rubber gasket bracelets on my wrist, a cropped

black leather Schott motorcycle jacket. I was looking at a full-length fun house version of myself, living and breathing, tall and narrow as a blade.

"See?" she beamed, her eyes wide with delight. "If you won't dress like me, then I will dress like you."

She backed up, sucked in her cheeks, sank her hands deep into her pockets, and spun around on one heel, exactly the way she did in the showroom.

. . .

EVERY WEEK BEFORE MY THERAPY appointment, I stop at an Italian restaurant with damp, sticky floors. The place—West Eighty-Sixth Street, all glass and mirrors and black enamel—is empty; "Hungry Like the Wolf" blasts on the sound system. It is late in the afternoon, any Thursday at four, 1988. Every week for the better part of five years, I arrive for my appointment an hour early, climb onto a barstool, and drink two fishbowl goblets of screw-top René Junot white wine. Because it is happy hour, I leave a ten-dollar bill for the two drinks. I thank the bartender, cross the street to a Gothic prewar apartment building, ring a buzzer, sit down on my therapist's brown corduroy couch, and stare out the window toward Riverside Drive and the Hudson River in the distance. Cars honk. I am certain that Anna, seated on an old brown Eames recliner and separated from me by its ottoman, will not notice, even though my breath stinks like the 5:07 Metro North bar car to Greenwich.

I drag my fingers back and forth along the worn fabric of

the couch; it is starting to lose its nap. My fingertips tingle. The feeling drains out of my hands; they are numb and heavy. I forget where I am. My legs wobble; my feet go cold and I can't feel the couch beneath me. I can't form words. I begin to shiver. I can see, across the ottoman, that Anna's lips are moving, but I can't make out what she's saying. She sounds like a record played on the wrong speed.

On this particular afternoon, Anna and I enter the territory of psychopathology, maternal grief, metabolization of long-term trauma, the DSM-III, and *Invasion of the Body Snatchers*.

"She was wearing the same clothes as me when she opened the door."

"So if you won't agree to be her, then she'll have to be you."

"That's right."

"So your life is not your own. You're the same person."

"Yes."

"And if you're a different person, she will hate you for abandoning her."

Yes.

"Do you ever think about having a family of your own? Maybe a child? What would that look like for you?"

I stare out the window. It's dark now; rush hour. The lights in Fort Lee, across the river, are beginning to twinkle.

"Who are you?"

"I don't know."

"Have you ever known?"

"I don't know."

13

"IT'S A MOTHER'S HEART," SHE WHINES. SHE LOOKS DOWN AT the table and blinks slowly. Her eyes fill with tears.

"What the hell is that supposed to mean?" I ask, shaking out my napkin.

She points to the top slice of black Russian pumpernickel holding my smoked salmon and cucumber sandwich together. I move it to the bread plate. My mother's slice-of-bread rule: one or none.

We are having lunch together at a restaurant a few blocks from my office. She has walked south down Broadway and east on Central Park South, stopping at Bergdorf, all the way from her apartment on the Upper West Side. On this day in 1997, we've met in the middle. She usually comes to the breezeway downstairs from my office, but I've been giving her excuses to meet me elsewhere. Lately, she's been flirting with the building security guard who lets her upstairs to see my gorgeous boss, Sloane, whose outfits she loves; I come back from the ladies' room, and there will be my mother, standing in my office, in conversation with lovely, beautiful Sloane, who is too polite to extricate herself. I blame it on a last-minute meeting, construction on the ground floor of my building, a need to stretch my legs after sitting all morning at my desk, where I am working as an editor.

"It's a mother's heart—" she says over lunch. "It's killing Bea. Lance is her only son."

She does the dramatic shiver. Her eyes are closed, she gives her head a quick twitch as if she's having a short seizure.

"Did you know?" she asks. She cocks her head like a puppy.

"Of course I knew—"

I motion to the server. I order a glass of wine, breaking my no-alcohol-at-lunch rule. My mother scowls.

"So why didn't you tell me?"

"Because it's nobody's business but his. Lance is a grown man. He's a lawyer—"

"But it's her *son*—it's her heart."

"What does that even *mean*? It's not like he's committed murder. He's *gay*—"

"Shut *up*," she whispers, cutting me off. Her nostrils flare. "Just shut *up*, you're making a scene."

My mother's eyes dart to the next table. She mouths *I'm sorry* to two young suited guys in their twenties, engrossed in quiet conversation, not looking at her. A diversionary tactic meant to result in shame; it is an implication to the outside world that her lunch date—her daughter—is crazy or ill-mannered or both, and that neighboring diners are disturbed by my bad behavior. *I'm sorry for her behavior,* the diversion says. *She's not well. I know . . . me too. I'm so embarrassed for her too.* Often, I look over to the recipient of her apology, and the table is empty.

"You're shushing me because I said Lance is gay?"

"Can you please not say it so loud?"

Her eyes dart from side to side.

"You're the one who asked—"

She pouts. We eat in silence. I pick at my pumpernickel. She shakes her head. She processes the news that this man—a close friend's son—prefers men to women.

"So does he have a friend or something?"

My mother cannot bring herself to say it: partner, boyfriend, girlfriend. *Lover,* which means there's sex involved, makes her head explode. So it's *friend:* Lance has a friend.

"His name is Dragon. They met on a cruise."

She stares at me over her breadless turkey and pesto sandwich.

"Bea's son has a friend named Dragon? Lance and Dragon?"

"He's from Croatia."

"Not Jewish?"

"First it's the end of the world that he's gay and now you're worried that his boyfriend isn't Jewish?"

"I don't believe it," she says, shaking her head. "Maybe he could change, for the right girl. I'm sure he's just bisexual, like Paul. It would just take a good woman."

A drop of pesto clings to her lips.

"He's not going to change, Ma, so don't even go there. And Paul is gayer than Liberace."

"He is *not*. I know he's interested in me. I catch him watching me all the time."

"He's just looking at your makeup," I say.

"He wants to go out with me—even Ben says so."

"Paul's had a partner for twenty-five years. He's your accompanist. You're paying him by the hour—"

. . . *like a hooker,* I mumble.

"What did you say?"

"Nothing—"

"It's a terrible thing," she says, shaking her head, her eyes filling with tears. "It's a mother's heart."

"It's his *life,* goddammit—"

"He can wait till she's dead. And then she won't know."

"She could live to be a hundred—"

"That's *his* problem."

. . .

IN MY EARLY THIRTIES, TEN years after being not quite in the closet and not quite out—*Your closet has a revolving door,* my friends said—I fled with a vengeance. I told cousins, close friends, some colleagues. A mentor from college, who had become a good, trusted friend.

"Does your mother know?" she asked.

"No," I said. "Not yet."

"Of *course* she knows," she said. "How could she *not* know? She's your *mother.*"

I told my father and Shirley over Indian food on Third Avenue. Tears spontaneously erupted from my eyes; I couldn't control them. My father got up from the other side of the table, sat down next to me, and took me in his arms.

"Does your mother know yet?" he asked.

"No—" I said.

"You have to tell her," he said. "You're a *separate person*— she needs to know that, to understand it."

I took her out to lunch the following week. We gaped at each other coldly over bowls of salad and long, narrow bread sticks. She stared at my hair. She ordered a glass of wine. I drank water.

"Mom—" I said. "I have to tell you something."

I wept; she knew.

"Are you telling me you're gay?"

I nodded.

"I'm sorry, Mom—"

"It's not possible," she said. "I didn't raise you that way."

"I'm sorry—"

"Do you have to look like Fran Lebowitz?"

"*What*—?"

"I know you like suits. This is your *father's* fault—"

"*I can't even*—"

"Does he know?"

"Yes—"

Her face turned purple.

"So you told *him* before you told *me*?"

No one—not family or friends or colleagues—had known about the brief, intense relationship I had with my roommate,

Julie, years earlier. That we had been gifted the keys to a friend's cabin in New Hampshire and, driving north into a blinding snowstorm, arrived, built a fire in the wood-burning stove, got into bed, and never left. No one knew that she could not tolerate the thought of being involved with a woman and brought man after man home to our apartment while I lay in the guest room on the other side of the wall, listening to them fuck like bunnies.

I was madly in love with her. I was gay. Julie, however, was not; she was experimenting. One day I came home from work to find her sitting on our couch sipping a cup of herbal tea, her dog-eared copy of Shakti Gawain's *Creative Visualization* by her side. A rose quartz geode the size of a cantaloupe glimmered on the maple Conran end table next to her; Windham Hill's *December* played on our tape deck; clouds of patchouli incense filled the air. Her blue eyes were wet. Before I had a chance to take my coat off, she said she'd had enough; she was ready to get on with her life. Hers was the primary name on our lease; when it was up, she would be moving to San Francisco to do an AIDS research fellowship. I needed to be out within the month. I had no money, no apartment, and nowhere to go. She gave me a small black velvet sack of rainbow tourmaline to purify my heart chakra. She gave me the cats.

The night that Julie asked me to leave, I took a taxi to my mother's apartment. We ordered Chinese takeout. We stood in the kitchen drinking white wine, and I lied that the woman she knew only as my roommate was going back to Nebraska to be closer to her family. She knitted her brow; she was poised for a fight. She didn't need to know anything else about us; she didn't need to know that I loved someone who wasn't her.

"So you can come *here*," my mother said. "You can live here again with me and Ben, darling. You don't need that whore anyway."

She pronounced it *who-a*: a Brooklyn, old-country way.

"She's not a whore, Mom—why would you even call her that?" I said.

My mother categorized people in the binary: friend, enemy. If she was no longer my friend, then she was my enemy. A low-life. Trash.

A whore.

"You should never have moved out of this apartment," she said. "*That* was your first mistake."

"It was for my own health, Mom—" I said.

"That's bullshit. You just *hate* me—" Her face began to flush. "The doctor turned you against me. And that Haffner shrink of yours. *I* know the truth."

"I can't move back in with you and Ben—"

"Of course you can—you just don't want to."

"I'm twenty-eight years old, Mom. I can't live with you—"

"I lived with Gaga until I met your father. I was twenty-six—"

"I'm not talking about you, Mom," I said. "I'm talking about me."

"You're never talking about me," she said. "It's always about you—"

"I'm sorry, Mom—" I said.

"I'll buy you a fur coat—"

"I don't want a fur coat, Mom. I hate fur."

"I have given you *everything*—You don't *know* what I gave up for you. Your goddamned father took everything from me and now, who are you? Miss PETA? So where are you going to go? Who else could you *possibly* have in your life?"

14

BEEP: *SO THE PLANE IS MISSING. CALL ME.*

Beep: *A search party. This is terrible. Good thing that Jackie's dead. Where the hell are you?*

Beep: *Her sister also. Cape Cod. Can't believe it. I asked you to call me.*

Beep: *The wedding, it's off. That Carolyn is such a ferbisinah. He had to marry someone with his sister's name? I am your mother. I am not dead. Call me.*

Beep: *So do you want to go to P.J. Clarke's? I'm going to Bloomie's. I'll meet you in the lobby in an hour.*

Beep: *Stop playing these games with me. I'm calling the police already.*

———

I apply the mascara first. I go over my eyelashes with the wand again and again, slowly, carefully, until my eyes are glued nearly shut as they might be with sickness, obscured by a waxy black debris that flakes off onto my cheekbones; I can barely see. My lips are engorged; they are dry and hot. I swipe on a bright red lipstick, again and again, around and around, covering my mouth, philtrum, chin, until the entire tube is gone, the stick worn flat to a scarlet button. I powder my face with a cobwebbed lamb's wool ball of the sort that might be stuffed into a ballerina's toe shoe. It is stapled into a yellow Bakelite handle crazed with time; the wool smells like corn silk. The puff is the size of a round bed pillow. I powder and powder until clouds of grayish pink dust fill the air around me. I cough. I brush my hair back with Gaga's long-handled dressing table brush, encrusted with rhinestones and strands of long white hair matted into its bristles. I turn to look in the lovely mirror that hangs over my dresser—it is white and pink, with dainty antique roses hand-painted between each of the drawer's round wooden handles; it is part of a set that includes a canopy bed, which my mother's father gave to me the year that he died—and what looks back is not human. Yellow and gray and pink, its eyes glued shut with hardening black paste, its lips polished until the blood-red scarlet wax coats the underside of the nose, which hangs like a boneless chicken breast, ugly and flaccid, over the mouth.

The moment in sleep when it is impossible to move, as though one has been pumped with curare: sleep paralysis. It presages in mythology what sleep scientists call the Night Hag Attack and its related hallucinations, voices, terrors, which occur, according to sleep specialists, during the hypnagogic, parasomniac stage. On this day in 1999, this makeup monster, half-living, half-dead, stares back at me from my childhood mirror. It is an overlay, a maternal triptych, a golem: my mother and Gaga and me, young and old, then and now, past and future.

I wake to find Viola, my tuxedo cat, sitting on my chest, cleaning my eyes, my lips, my cheeks, my hair, as if I were a kitten. Cleo, my Siamese, is nestled against the small of my back, asleep. I'm not sure of the time. The track lights above my sleigh bed are on. The answering machine is beeping; I hear my mother's voice. Something about John-John. A truck outside on Fifty-Eighth Street is going in reverse.

Days earlier.

I have taken the crosstown bus to the Upper West Side in order to feed a friend's new poodle puppy; my friend has gotten stuck at her job downtown and can't get back to her apartment in time to change the newspaper she's put down in her kitchen, to play with the pup, to feed and water her. I pick up my friend's keys from the man she's been sleeping with—he's married; he can't be seen going into her apartment himself; the neighbors are gossiping—and I let myself in. I climb over the plastic baby gate that keeps Laverne in the kitchen and peeing on the paper that has been set down on the kitchen floor. I clean everything up. I put down fresh paper. I feed her. I throw a small stuffed moose across the room for her again and again; she doesn't tire of the game and retrieves it for an hour until it's a damp, sucked-upon mess and she is exhausted. I get up to leave and feel dizzy. I drink a glass of cold water. I sit down on the floor with Laverne, who is pleased that I've decided to stay. I wake up two hours later, the gray speckled linoleum cool against my back, pinned down by a small, furry weight. Laverne is stretched out on top of me, her little black nose resting on my chest.

I take a taxi home, across Central Park and down to Fifty-Seventh Street. I put dishes of food down for my cats, wet and dry, and fill their water bowl. I kick off my sandals, pull the covers back on my bed, and pass out in my clothes.

For the coming days, I will sleep and wake at six-hour intervals. When my temperature hits one hundred and four, I take two Tylenol, which will bring the fever down fast enough for me to get up and change my soaked sheets, pull a fresh T-shirt out of my drawer and put it on, and climb back into bed. I sleep and sleep; when the Tylenol wears off, a violent rattling wakes me, my skin burning and sore to the touch as if I have been baked on a hot dry stone.

The illness—sudden, untraceable; this is the middle of summer and not flu season—is a purge, an emetic. I am releasing something. I have carried it with me like a bucket, heavy with mud, and with every step my health has dimmed. I am sick. I am alone. The phone is ringing; the Kennedys.

I am your mother. I am not dead. Call me.

I will not call. I let it go.

A shift; I will leave New York, or I will die.

· · ·

WEEKS EARLIER:

We had been sitting on my friend's couch in North Carolina,

not far from Chapel Hill. I had traveled south from New York to attend a small literary festival. Laura, whom I had known during the summers of my sleepaway camp childhood in Pennsylvania—she had been my counselor for seven years— lived close by and worked at the university. I found her email address through a random search after hearing that she was living there and working in academia. We were in touch for the first time in decades.

I wrote; she wrote back. We spoke as though no time had passed. We talked about jobs lost and found. About moving with Jennifer, her partner of two decades, from Texas to Georgia to North Carolina. Rounding the corner in her life where she had spent more time living with her partner than not, she spoke in befores and afters. The challenges of living as gay women in a region that is still, in some pockets, small-minded and relentless in its bigotry. She asked if I was single; I said I was. She asked for my mother.

Is she still so beautiful? she wrote. *I remember her on visiting day. None of the other mothers looked like her. She seemed completely out of place, disoriented. I remember you crying when she arrived with your father. Nobody else cried when their mothers arrived.*

She's still beautiful, I wrote back.

We talked about camp, and that it seemed to be another lifetime ago. That every day after dinner, when the other girls were playing tennis or meeting boys behind the camp laundry, she would watch me hike into the vast fields behind girls' campus that abutted a local dairy farm overgrown at its edges with lamb's quarters and chickweed. I would sit on the ground, up to my shoulders in tall grass, obscured, watching the cows graze just beyond the fence. I was drawn to the silence and the quiet, a place where my head could be clear. My mother had warned her that at home I had become moody and glum and asked her to keep an eye on me; I seemed to have retreated into myself.

I flew down to Raleigh-Durham and Laura picked me up at the airport on a hot June day.

We hugged and took a step back so that we could get a better look at each other. I was in my early thirties; she was in her early forties. She hadn't changed, apart from a few strands of graying dark hair.

As a teenager, Laura had always been kind and warm, but not willing to take any bullshit from her young, hormonal, often obnoxious charges; she exuded competence and self-possession even at sixteen. I knew, in the wordless way that one does, a particular *unknown known*: that she was somehow different, and so was I. When we reconnected as adults, I came out to her on a long hike with Jennifer and their dogs in the hills outside of Chapel Hill.

Well, of course, she said.

I knew about you forever, we both said.

When? we asked simultaneously.

Always, we answered.

We stopped at a brook to let the animals swim.

"So is there anyone?" she asked.

There isn't, I told her.

"Anyone you're interested in?"

I'm not.

"Dating?"

Not really.

"Sex?"

Sometimes.

"Why?"

I threw a stick for one of the dogs.

"It's so beautiful down here," I said to her that night. We were sitting on her couch drinking glasses of wine while Jennifer made dinner. It was quiet, apart from an army of peepers loud enough to be heard in the next state.

"There's a lot of work down here," she said. "It's cheaper than New York—"

"Everything is cheaper than New York—"

"Why don't you think about moving? We'll help—"

"I can't—" I said, quickly.

It was instant; a reflexive *no,* like stepping on a tack.

"Why not?"

"Because I can't abandon her—"

The words hung in the air between us. Laura shook her head.

"Liss," she said, "you are never going to meet anyone until your heart is ready to leave."

I know, I said.

"It's time for you to have your own life."

I know.

"It's time for you to go—"

15

MY MOTHER IS SHARING A HOSPITAL ROOM WITH A LONG-HAIRED Mongolian woman in her forties who is dying from stomach cancer. An assortment of people have flown in from the other side of the world to translate, to hold the woman's hand, to sit vigil night and day with her while decisions are made: If she can survive the flight, can she return to Ulaanbaatar to die at home, or will she return to the small apartment in Flushing that she shares with six other women, for hospice care? There is no money for continued treatment; there is no insurance.

"The other women will help," someone says.

"Are there any children?" a hospital administrator asks.

Doctors, residents, interns, clipboards in hand, all want to know who is the responsible party.

No, the people around her keep answering: *No children. Alone.*

"It's like Grand Central Station in here," my mother whispers to me, lowering the volume on her television. "The poor thing—it's so depressing that they can't do anything for her—she's up all night. They should put her in a private room. It scares me that she is alone."

My mother reaches up for my hand and elevates her bed so she can see a bit better.

She is neither alive nor dead, this young woman in the bardo who floats in and out of consciousness, between two worlds. My mother is terrorized by her proximity to the unknown; she can't control it, can't manipulate it, can't pretty it up. After I leave, she throws a full bedpan; she asks for Xanax; she asks to be moved; she files a complaint against an aide who doesn't instantly respond to her; she squeezes the call buzzer for hours until the nurse's station, monitoring her remotely, disconnects it; she self-soothes and calls the Clinique counter at Saks to order hundreds of dollars' worth of a pale lavender face milk, to be delivered to her bed in the hospital. I have her wallet but the salesgirl has her credit card on file. The fact of the situation in her midst, of the seeming hopelessness of it all—a young woman, alone, dying just a few feet away from her in a strange hospital in a strange place, an anonymous body in this sterile universe of gauze and suture—renders my mother hysterical. She can't get up and walk away, walk anywhere, walk to Saks, walk home.

"But she is not alone, Ma," I say. "She has people with her at all times."

A tribe standing watch over the woman has assembled to talk to her in the words she knows—*untaakh,* they say like a mother to her baby; *sleep, sleep*—to make sure that when she opens her eyes, someone is always there. What could possibly have more meaning as one draws one's last breath than *this*: They have come to help ease her way.

"But no children," my mother says, her eyes wide with panic. "No children."

She grabs my hands in hers and strokes them while she stares wide-eyed and unblinking at Perry Mason on the television attached to the place where the ceiling meets the wall. He looks down at her from the heavens, like a god.

"Don't leave," she begs. "Promise me you won't leave."

My mother's hands are ice-cold, white as marble, bruised in flowers of green and brown from the emergency room intravenous lines, shaking.

"I won't, Ma," I say. "I promise."

. . .

"DO YOU THINK YOUR MOTHER might want to talk to someone?" Brittney, the hospital social worker asks. "From the pastoral office?"

"She's not religious," I say. I am leaving for the day, standing at the nurse's station.

"But sometimes it helps?"

"If you send her a priest, she'll drop dead on the spot," I say, rolling my eyes.

"I don't get it," she says, smiling uncomfortably. "Is that a joke?"

"Never mind," I say. "It's fine."

I like Brittney: She brings my mother cookies, which my mother loves and eats like a child under the covers when no one is watching—an orderly frets about the crumbs—and sneaks her a mesclun salad with nuts and raisins from a nearby bistro. My mother lights up in Brittney's presence; they share magazines and Hollywood gossip. George Clooney's wife is too smart for him. Melania's outfits are getting too conservative. Coats like Pat Nixon.

I agree; don't you? they say to each other.

Brittney comes to see her when she's off her shift and it's time to leave. A young woman with kind brown eyes and straight dark hair, she is possessed of a taut body that has responded to hours of the Pilates she has regularly fed it at one of the nearby studios on the Upper East Side. I can see her stretched out long and lean on a reformer, dressed in black Lululemon tights and a bright white tank, her new pink-gold Apple watch reflecting the glint of sun streaming into the room through ceiling-height windows facing Madison Avenue. She is fresh-faced and energetic, a platinum wedding band encrusted with baguette diamonds gracing her slender left hand. A dozen red roses are delivered to her desk near the nurse's station twice a week.

"Tell me about your fella," my mother says to her. "I wanna hear about your fella."

Brittney's life will unfold. A prediction: She has married an associate in a downtown entertainment law firm. In six months, they will move from their one-bedroom rental on the Upper East Side, Ninetieth Street, to Brooklyn Heights, a prewar co-op a few blocks from the Promenade, where they will walk their teacup French bulldog every morning and evening. A baby will arrive, and two years later they will decamp for northern Westchester, Katonah, for its lovely small-town feel and train accessibility. Brittney will open a private therapy practice once the second baby is three and the two children go off to day school. They will add a yellow Labrador retriever and a calico cat to the family. Christmases and Easters will be crowded affairs and include both sets of grandparents, siblings and their families, stray friends from college with nowhere to go. There will be family vacations every year, a cancer scare that will prove to be, thank God, nothing. By the time Brittney is sixty-five, she will be a grandmother twice over, married for what seems like forever, summering every year in a rambling shingled cottage on the midcoast of Maine. Big enough to have everyone there all at once, it will be outfitted with wheelchair ramps for Brittney's ninety-two-year-old mother, who comes up from Vero Beach to stay every summer with her caregiver.

Is Brittney twenty-eight? Thirty?

Every morning, Brittney strolls the halls in staggeringly high heels, clipboard in hand, starched and ironed, perfectly but not overly made up, not a strand of hair out of place. I imagine that she has just finished breakfast: a kale, cucumber, parsley juice with a double shot of ginger and turmeric to bolster her immune system. She weighs nothing. She is lovely and earnest and will be with my mother only for another week: She is going on maternity leave. I never notice the small baby bump obscured by her white coat until she mentions it.

When I arrive on this particular morning, the Mongolian woman is asleep, morphine dripping into her arm. An older man and woman sit in chairs near the door, reading; they nod to me; I nod back. Brittney is perched on the end of my mother's bed near the window, reviewing the contents of my mother's makeup bag the way young boys review baseball cards. I watch them for a moment from the doorway, the sunlight behind them; they are forehead to forehead looking down at the bedcover and its pile of treasure. My mother unscrews a bright red lipstick and holds it up, as if to say, *This one, this color changed everything.* Brittney nods and smiles; they throw their heads back and laugh together. She swipes it across the back of her hand and cocks her head to the side.

They don't see me. I am a witness to what might have been, what *could* have been, like in a scene from Dickens: *The ghost of Christmas yet to come.*

Brittney is the daughter my mother should have had. She is the twin. Dread and jealousy boil up in me like a pot on high. *Why couldn't I have been this woman for my mother?*

I cough and my mother looks up and waves energetically, her IV lines dancing around the side of her bed. She beams; I bring her mail, the newspapers, a latte from the Starbucks kiosk in the lobby. I kiss her hello on the top of her head, the way I did to my kids when I was a counselor in sleepaway camp.

"Good morning, darling—" she says. She stops, pulls back for a moment, screws up her eyes. "Let me see your shoes—"

"She's *totally* fabulous," Brittney whispers as we walk out to the nurse's station together.

"She is," I say.

"She said the hospital got it wrong and she's sixty," she says. "*Really*—I said to her, *then why do you have Medicare*—and she told me to be a pal and lie for her. *Can you imagine?*"

"That sounds about right," I sigh.

"It must be so amazing for you," she says. "She loves you so much."

"It is," I say, smiling. "Totally. I love her too."

"But it must be hard—she says she's a walker. That it's her thing. We have to make sure that she can still do it when she gets out of rehab. I'm worried that she's getting depressed. She's not eating."

"She doesn't eat," I say, "as a rule."

"Nothing?"

"Rarely," I say.

Her face grows serious. We talk about what's next: Where she will go to rehab. What her insurance will pay for and what they won't. Where the financial burden will lie. How she will fare with the exercises. Will her bones be strong enough to support her body, which is fueled on plain white diet bread and an egg white and a few ounces of chicken, probably fewer than a thousand calories a day.

"If walking the city is the motivator," I tell Brittney, "she will do the exercises. She has to be able to walk again; if she doesn't, it will kill her."

Her face grows solemn; she nods. She understands. *Solvitur ambulando.*

Brittney wants to know: My mother said she was Jewish when she arrived in the emergency room. Perhaps she would like to see a rabbi? Perhaps, she says, a visit might provide her with some existential comfort?

. . .

IN 1974, THE YEAR OF my new womanhood, my parents sent me to camp in Pennsylvania, where I would spend eight weeks. The day after I left, they flew to Britain and Europe for two weeks: London, Paris, Vienna, Florence, Rome, home. At every stop, my mother bought souvenirs: Mary Quant makeup on Carnaby Street. Victorian cherry amber at the Place Clignancourt in Paris. Viennese wooden carvings to hang in the living room. A cameo that she swears looks exactly like me, hand-painted by an artist who sold them outside the Duomo. Two sets of rosary beads at the Vatican: one for my mother's friend Olga, an Italian woman who lived in our building, and one for her. She bought them and held them up in front of the window when the pope appeared. She wanted them to be blessed, to be sanctified by the man with an inside track.

"I had a big fight with your father about it," she told me when I got home from camp. She held the rosaries up: tiny black and silver beads ending in small silver crucifixes. "Your father said, *So what are you becoming now? A Catholic?*"

She deposited them in my tiny hands and I rolled them around and felt the cool black stone of each bead. I ran my finger along the narrow, tortured body of Jesus from his feet to his crown of thorns. I gave them back to her.

"Do you wear them?" I asked. "Like a necklace?"

"No," she said, "I don't *think* so. We're Jews—"

"So why did you buy them?"

"For *luck,*" she shrugged. "Because everyone needs a little luck. *I* need a little luck."

She smiled and tucked them back into her jewelry box; I never saw them again.

Years later, a huge laughing Buddha—*Hotei the eccentric—*

showed up on the piano, situated between her silver loving cup and my tennis awards; every morning before she and Ben left for work, she rubbed the deity's bright red belly—the color red wards off the evil eye in Jewish tradition—and made a wish for health and prosperity. When her neighbor came back from a trip to Israel, she brought my mother a massive mezuzah to affix to her front door; the size of a box of Tiparillos and the color of bone, it was decorated in a relief depicting the anguished, twisted bodies of the Holocaust—mothers and children, older people and babies—memorialized at Yad Vashem, where the mezuzah was purchased. I gasped when I saw it.

"It's just modern," my mother said when I asked if she knew anything about it and understood what it represented: destruction and survival, parents and children.

She kisses her mezuzah both going and coming: on her way out of her apartment and always on her way in. Susan and I were mezuzahless for a year, when we had our siding replaced and the workmen accidentally broke it—a Murano glass mezuzah brought back for us by my father from the Jewish ghetto in Venice. I kept it, broken in two, in my jewelry box—so when my mother came to visit, she simply pretended that it was still there. She kissed her hand, reached up, and touched the unadorned door frame. Invisible to everyone but her, it contained the *klaf,* the scroll on which appear verses from Deuteronomy, commanding that *His word be inscribed on the doorposts of thy house and upon thy gates.* My mother harangued me until I bought a replacement and attached it in time for her next visit.

It's unlucky not to have one, she said.

"Do you even know what it means," I said.

For a while in the eighties and nineties, she lit my grandmother's Sabbath wedding candlesticks on Friday nights because Ben had asked her to, the way his own mother, who had been observant, did; my mother blew them out after he went to bed. Once Ben died, she split the set up and stuck a leopard print candle in the one that she stood on the piano next to her loving cup, like a beacon.

What *is* luck: a flimsy manifestation of a religion for the secularly ambivalent and the superstitious? Is it hope? The result of a favorable or unfavorable view of a particular deity?

"What did I do to deserve this?" my mother cried the night of her accident. "I am so *good* to people. I have such terrible luck. God hates me."

"You were *so* lucky," I told her, "that the one doctor in America who is an expert at repairing your kind of injury, at what is the best orthopedic hospital in the world, which happens to be located in the city in which you live, was on call that night."

"If I was lucky," she said, "this wouldn't have happened at all."

In my childhood home, she fends off bad spirits at every turn: the evil eye, *poo poo poo, kenorahorah,* knock on wood, toss a penny in a fountain, salt over a shoulder, step on a crack, the warding off of the devil. Over the years, she wears an Egyptian ankh, a Brazilian figa, an Italian horn of plenty, a Chinese articulated fish painted with green enamel, Gaga's green jade beads, a brooch in the shape of a lucky frog brought back from Puerto Rico, a red string on her wrist, and in her purse a trio of highly polished stones carved on one side in English and the

other in Hebrew with the words HEALTH PROSPERITY HAPPI-
NESS that Lucille brought her from the Kabbalah Center back
when Madonna was a member. All of them are meant to bring
her good fortune, to assure her safety, long life, money. To give
her the things she wants.

None of them promises love.

16

"I ASSUME SHE WILL BE GOING HOME WITH YOU?"

My mother's rehab case manager smiles at me across the ersatz walnut conference room table where I sit, sandwiched between Susan and the attorney we have hired. Betty's hands are clasped tightly in front of her, her nails filed short and square and decorated with small purple and white unicorn appliqués; each of the creature's ten eyes is fashioned from a single drop of lavender glitter that sparkles under the fluorescent ceiling lights. She is wearing gold half glasses on the end of her nose and a large gold cross around her neck; the corners of her yellow cardigan are clipped together with a short pearloid chain. A manila folder with my mother's name written in red Magic Marker sits in front of her on top of a blank legal pad. We are meeting to discuss my mother's insurance situation, which is, Betty says, terrible.

Most rehab patients who are in their seventies and beyond have traditional Medicare plus supplemental insurance for which they pay a monthly fee. Together, the combination results in medical bills being, in most cases, nominal. But when my mother turned sixty-five in 2000, she decided against carrying the traditional Medicare card because it would instantly reveal her age. And a supplement, she reasoned, would tap her monthly expendable cash, which she was using for other things. Planning for the future, for the probability and likelihood of illness, simply never figured in.

We fought; she railed. *You don't understand my needs.*

"But what will you do if you have an accident?" I asked.

"I'll sell something," she said. "Just like I did when your father went bankrupt."

Seventeen years later, we sit here, in an airless conference room at a for-profit rehab center, face-to-face with Betty.

"We need to look at our options," she says, smiling at us across the table. "I understand that you two girls live in a ranch house."

. . .

MY MOTHER IS UPSTAIRS IN her room, where she has been for five days, since her release from the hospital. It is Christmas. Her left foot is encased in a black plastic knee-high cam boot, her right foot in a shorter one. She has not stood or walked for more than two weeks, and her legs are beginning to atrophy, her flesh turning to putty. On this day, she sits up in her bed, fully made up like Norma Desmond, wrapped up in an Italian wool paisley shawl like a grand pasha, wearing the PolarFleece leopard print pants we bought for her when she arrived without any pajamas. Her black long-sleeved T-shirt says *Queen for a day* in rhinestone script.

Every afternoon, Juan, the gay facility janitor, makes the rounds dressed as Santa Claus. If my mother is in a good mood, she looks forward to his arrival.

"Have you been a very good girl this year?" Juan asks as I walk into her room—a single near the nurse's station, where the facility administrator thought she would be most comfortable.

"Get the fuck out of my room, Santa," my mother says. "My sugar's dropping. Get me a cookie."

"Merry Christmas," Santa grumbles. He heads to the nurse's station to find my mother a cookie.

"You can't say *fuck* to Santa, Ma—" I say, putting down a bag of magazines on her swing-away table: *Vogue, Harper's Bazaar, Allure, Marie Claire, Vanity Fair, Elle, Elle Décor, New York,* and her favorite coffee table book about the Kennedys.

"I want a fucking cookie," she says, reaching up for me with both arms. "You look tired—" She squints and checks me out, up and down.

"I *am* tired, Ma—"

"So you should sleep more. It's not like you should come here every day or anything. I'll be fine without you."

I bend down to kiss her. She grabs my hand. I pull it away.

"You need your highlights," she says, fingering my hair. "You'll look less tired."

The television is on. *It's a Wonderful Life.* Donna Reed is hanging wallpaper.

"When I can get to it," I say.

"Get to it," she says. *"Make the time."*

We have moved her from the hospital in Manhattan to a rehabilitation center in Connecticut ten minutes from our house so that I can be her advocate—*She'll need an advocate,* Brittney said, *and that should be you*—and the facility knows that there is always someone there, always watching when the mistakes, which are plentiful and dangerous, are made: The attempts at giving her pills for a condition she doesn't have. The lack of an identification bracelet for more than twenty-four hours after her arrival. My mother's hysterical allergy to pink serves her well: On a middle-of-the-night visit by an inept nurse's aid, she refuses blood pressure medication meant for another patient simply based on its color, and saves her own life.

I visit her every day, twice a day, at the beginning. I bring her what she wants, making lists of the things that will make her most comfortable. She spends her days in bed watching television, a bulging flowered Clinique makeup bag tucked up under each armpit. Each morning an orderly brings her a plastic basin of water so that she can wash her face and apply fresh makeup; every afternoon she removes it and reapplies it. On this day, she decides she needs a new supply from her stash in her apartment. She sends me back to the city for a few things.

"Go into the hallway bathroom," she instructs as I sit on the end of her bed, a pen and pad on my lap. "There's Clinique powder on the bottom shelf of the vanity. You could bring me that."

"Anything else?" I ask.

"In my bedroom bathroom, there are a few tubes of lipstick in Red Red Red. I could use those. I'm running low."

"How could you be running low? You're in a rehab."

She throws her head back and screams, a sudden, ear-piercing shriek like an infant's; her face changes color.

"Because I *need* them because I wear my makeup *every damn day* I want to die kill me just *kill me* my life is *over*—"

She weeps and shrieks and her cell phone rings and she answers it and it's Dick and she cries to him, cries that *everything* is over, everything that she has worked so hard for has been taken away from her and she has nothing else to live for and she just wants to die.

"Is she okay?" an orderly asks, poking her head in.

"Fine," I say.

Susan and I drive into the city; we turn it into a date night. Dinner at Buvette, where we had been married in the tiny courtyard a few years earlier, and where we asked the chef, Jody Williams, to cook whatever she wanted to make. Friends and family came; my mother sat at the head of the table. Platters of French comfort food arrived: roast chicken and herbs, green beans vinaigrette. Rosé was poured, bottle after bottle. Our wedding cake was a tarte Tatin. *I'm happy,* my mother said, as Susan and I sliced through the layers of caramelized apple and sweet, buttery pastry.

At the apartment, we look for my mother's makeup. Susan takes my mother's bathroom; I take the hallway powder room.

"Can you come here for a minute?" Susan yells from the bedroom bathroom.

Lined up in her medicine cabinet like Tory soldiers on the battlefield at Lexington are thirty-one tubes of Clinique lipstick in various stages of light use. Some of them are still in their little green boxes, the silver tubes wrapped in sheets of flowered Kleenex.

In the hallway powder room, I get down on my hands and knees on the cold white tile and open the vanity doors. I find a brightly flowered zippered tote bag stuffed with fifteen plastic Clinique powder compacts, each one barely touched.

We do the math: more than a thousand dollars.

We sit down on her bed; I pick up the phone. My hands shake.

"Ma, we found your makeup. You have a problem—"

My throat closes up. I fight off tears. She's been found out. Her lifeline will be cut, the switch flipped. Without beauty, she will die. There will be addiction specialists, therapists, family meetings; she will be forced, at last, to tell the truth.

"Good—" she says. "So you'll bring them tomorrow?"

"Ma—we found thirty-one tubes of lipstick. And fifteen powder compacts—"

"That's right," she says. "Bring them all—"

"All of them?"

Susan mouths *All of them?*

"I might need them," she says. "*Why* can't you ever understand that."

The unendurable: the specific moment when I can hold her fear in my hands like a snow globe, and shake it, and turn it to the light, and see the pieces of her life fall like flakes. I will be the one to say *no*, to kill her, to rob her of her beauty, to give her over to time.

. . .

"YOUR HOME WILL BE ABSOLUTELY perfect for her," Betty says across the conference room table. "We can hook you up with Visiting Nurse and set you up."

"My client is not interested in what you think about her home," my attorney says. She is young, kind-faced, soft-spoken, take-no-prisoners.

Although Betty will not tell us how many days of rehab my mother's bare-bones insurance has agreed to cover, she has taken the initiative to Google-map my home to make an accessibility determination.

Susan and I have paid our attorney to obtain one single piece of information with which the rehab is not willing to part, and without which they can compel my mother—compel me—to agree to pay for her entire stay out of pocket, to keep her there, keep her safe, and teach her how to walk again so that she can get back to her life. How many days will they pay for before she is kicked out and sent home—to my home? to her home?—where she will need a round-the-clock caregiver to help her bathe, dress, do laundry, cook, get to and from appointments, none of which is covered by insurance.

How many days?

She'll be your responsibility.

———

Susan has measured the width of our hallway, our bathroom doors, the entrance to the guest room. None of them is wide enough to accommodate a wheelchair or a walker.

"We can get a transit chair if we have to," Susan says, making notes on a legal pad. "They're smaller. We'll need a riser for the toilet, and grab bars. Maybe a hospital bed for the den if we can't get her into the guest room."

I sit on the couch drinking Scotch.

I envision the two of us lifting my mother on and off the commode and wiping her like an infant once she's out of the Depends that she will refuse to wear during her recuperation. I see us settling her on a white plastic shower chair in our bathroom, one of us naked and washing her hair, her head tilted back like a little girl's, her eyes closed, water dripping off her body in beads. I see us riding in the jump seat of an ambulette hurtling toward Bloomingdale's and wheeling her through the makeup department, where she greets all the clerks. She looks up at me while I set the brake on her chair; she's wide-eyed and wanting, pleading for a fix. *I need a few new eye pencils,* I imagine her saying as her favorite saleswoman bends down to ask what she's looking for today.

"You don't have to do this," a social worker friend tells me. "It's not inevitable. There are places she can go."

"I can't," I tell her.

"You might have to," she says.

"We don't do that kind of thing in my family," I say.

When Gaga's mother was dying of emphysema in 1948, she was brought into my mother's childhood apartment along with an oxygen tank and tent. There was no question that she would live there and die there, which she did. When Susan's grandmother could no longer stay on her farm, she was moved into Susan's bedroom, where she lived until her death at 103. The human tribe; the smoothing of the way. The Mongolian woman whose people flew from the other side of the world to sit with her. The lowest common denominator of humanity.

"You might have to," my friend repeats. "It might be a matter of your health."

I envision it straight out of the movies my mother is obsessed with: She is sitting in a hallway, a city hospital, full makeup. She is wild-eyed, manic, restrained. I imagine them coming at her with a giant glass syringe, and she is weeping and swaying her head back and forth: *No no no no.* She is living and dying in filth because I, her only child, enjoying her settled middle-aged life in her tidy home in Connecticut, cannot have her move in with me, into a room that, in my dreams, might have been meant for a baby.

We sit across the conference room table, the cross around Betty's neck glimmering under the lights.

"Your mother is refusing to do any physical therapy," Betty says. "We asked her what she does want to do, and she says she just wants to lay in bed, play with her makeup, and watch television all day, like she does at home.

"This is a problem," Betty continues, "and if she doesn't start to show any interest in improving her situation, her insurance will cut her off."

"How many days, Betty?" I ask.

This is all we want to know in order to prepare, to change our lives, to find a way to welcome her in.

17

SUSAN AND I HAVE FALLEN IN LOVE WITH A SMALL, DISCREET farmhouse in Camden, Maine. It is perfect for us: not too much property, a fenced-in yard for the dog, a recently renovated kitchen that occupies the entire back of the house. Walkable to the beautiful village where we have many friends—Camden lies between lush Mount Battie and the great expanse of Penobscot Bay, the color of slate—the house feels *right*.

One early morning before seven, we harness Petey, pack hot coffee in our canteens, and hike to the top of the mountain. We are not in good shape, and much older people pass us coming down the trail without so much as a huff: An aching back has lately prevented me from running, and Susan's job requires her to be sedentary for most of the day. But parts of the hike are thoughtfully paved for people of every level, and done slowly, it becomes a walking meditation at the top of which is air and sea, for miles.

It is a weekday, well past tourist season, getting chilly. We face the harbor. Millay's words give my steps cadence; they dance in my head like a nursery rhyme: *All I could see from where I stood / Was three long mountains and a wood; / I turned and looked the other way / And saw three islands in a bay.* Strung together in the distance, pale as a bruise, lie Isleboro, Vinalhaven, North Haven. Lobster boats head out to pull in their traps. A line of sea kayakers snakes out into the water with a guide, weaving between three-masted tourist schooners and smaller sailboats, paddling their long, narrow boats against the current, heading for breakfast on Curtis Island; we will do this tomorrow after dinner tonight with dear friends we rarely get to see.

Neither of us says it, but we both know: After almost twenty years together, this is our next place, our next step. The third season of our lives.

We will make an offer on the little house in town.

Early on, the subject of our first conversations was *place;* the fact of it, and how it can translate into safety or danger, if only by association to love and event. Susan adored the Southwest, for the sky and the space. After a bad breakup in the eighties, she went on a vision quest trip to New Mexico; there was a hike with a sixty-pound pack, a three-day fast, a thunderstorm while she was camping at the top of a mountain in the Sangre de Cristos. We both loved Marin: the weather, the hills. I loved

Colorado; it was easy to be healthy there. She loved Seattle for the city and the water; her best friend from college lives in Friday Harbor. Susan once spent a month in the Pacific Northwest without her mother ever knowing. Helen hated it when her daughter just went in to Manhattan for a few hours; how could she possibly tolerate her only child being thousands of miles away for so long? Susan didn't tell her. She called her every morning from her cell phone as though she were right around the corner. A sin of omission. A matter of self-preservation.

Do you think less of me? she asked when she told me the story.

At the time, her mother was in her seventies and in good health. Susan knew how to love her mother but also protect herself. I didn't think less of her; I envied her.

When I met Susan, she kept a small stack of books on her nightstand: Donald Hall's *Without,* Jane Kenyon's *A Hundred White Daffodils,* M.F.K. Fisher's *Last House.*

"Don't think I'm a depressive," she laughed.

"I think you're just looking for home," I said. "What it's like to have it."

"Or not," she said.

It was early afternoon at the start of our life together; we dozed in bed, reading. I loved Kenyon's taut essays about the ordinary: her local five-and-dime, her garden, her move to Hall's ancestral New Hampshire home, becoming her church treasurer and not knowing how to balance her checkbook. Susan read Hall's elegy for his late wife, who had, he wrote, come into her beauty at forty *as into a fortune*. There was Fisher's last book, titled for the final place she lived after three marriages, a long writing career, caregiving a difficult aging parent, raising her children on her own. I dipped in and out of it; two chapters about her elderly father, "Rex I" and "Rex II," whiplash from delight in the older man's presence to venomous bile. *A light here requires a shadow there.*

The books stayed on Susan's table until we moved four years later, their spines cracked. *A triptych.* Love, loss, the passage of ordinary time.

The rooms in the little Camden farmhouse were suddenly too small, the stairway too narrow. It was seven hours from New York, and hard to get to. Would it be our last house? Could we grow older there?

If my mother came, would she—*could* she—ever leave?

We signed the papers and handed over the deposit and days later retracted it. I was not ready to go, and I would never cross the threshold again.

18

THE FIFTH COMMANDMENT, ACCORDING TO THE TALMUD AND the Shulchan Aruch, the Code of Jewish Law, and the New Testament: *Thou shalt honor thy mother and thy father, that your days may be long upon this land that God has given you.* The first commandment that comes with a promise, a condition attached to it by the apostle Paul while preaching to the Ephesians: *Be a good child throughout the course of your parents' life,* he says, *and you will find favor and dwell in the holy land.*

I don't dwell in the holy land; I dwell in Connecticut, in a small ranch house.

Dora, my mother's round-the-clock caregiver and a devout Christian, interprets the words for me while my mother naps in her den.

"The Holy Land is *your* holy land—the kingdom of your heart," Dora says. "Honor her and your heart will be saved."

Dora is a petite, pleasant woman, dressed in brightly colored surgical scrubs, the Jamaican-born mother of two grown sons she is putting through college. Susan and I have found her through an old sleepaway camp friend whose difficult father needed in-home care over the last four years of his life. During our interview over white ceramic bowls of café au lait at Pain Quotidien around the corner from Susan's office, Dora tells us that this is her calling, the reason why she was put on this earth: to care for the old, the infirm, the difficult.

"I am here," Dora says plainly, "to ease their pain, and yours."

"Bullshit artist?" I ask Susan after our meeting.

"I don't think so," Susan says.

. . .

DURING THE WEEKS MY MOTHER was in rehab, a wild-eyed, white-haired woman in her early nineties lived in a room down the hall from my mother's, near the elevators. She had fallen and broken a hip; the drugs had taken a toll and pitched her into a dementia that she hadn't arrived with. She experienced sundowning: late-day confusion, agitation, restlessness, suspicion, all exacerbated by surgery and medication, a change of place and atmosphere where the lights were on all the time and the voices in the hallway outside her room terrorized her. Every day, her daughter, a middle-aged woman, heavyset and prone to

panting—a bank teller and a single mom with two teenagers;
good kids, I heard her tell a nurse—arrived at her mother's bed-
side at exactly the same time. She spent hours grooming her
like a baby: She combed her mother's thinning silver hair. She
painted her mother's fingernails and clipped her hard, yellowing toenails. She applied her makeup, instructing her to *look
down* when it came time for the mascara, and to *purse your lips*
for the lipstick. Once the older woman was satisfied, her daughter covered her mother's legs with a woolen blanket and wheeled
her out into a bland fluorescent-lit common area decorated in
shades of mauve and cornflower blue, where together they
gazed out the window at the New England countryside. In a
little while, she wheeled her mother back to her room, settled
her in bed with the help of a nurse, fed her dinner, and left.
The next day and the day after that and the one that followed,
she did the same thing. This was their routine despite the fact
that the older woman no longer recognized her daughter. She
could have been an orderly or a nurse. A complete stranger.

One early evening, the bank teller and I stood together in
the lobby, still decorated for Christmas, looking through the
glass doors out at the parking lot; we considered the snow. We
put on hats and gloves and fished car keys out of bags. She was
weary; she sighed.

"I see you here all the time," she told me. "Your mother is a
very beautiful woman. It's clear how much you love each other."

"I wish I could do for her what you do for yours," I said. "I
hate this."

"Everyone hates this," she said. "I hate everything about it.
But when it's my turn, my children will do the same for me.
And yours will do the same for you."

. . .

"I HAVE AN APARTMENT," MY mother announced, "and I am going home to it."

Unable to stand, walk, bathe herself, make a cup of coffee, use the bathroom, organize her pills, or navigate her space in a wheelchair, my mother was released from rehab. An adjuster working for her insurance company and located in an office seven thousand miles away in Pakistan had decided, based on his review of Betty's documents, that it was safe for her to leave.

"Sorry," Betty said in a phone call, "your appeal for an extension of stay has been denied by your mother's insurance company. You need to get her in two days."

She wanted to go home; we were relieved. We didn't beg; we didn't argue. Her doctors were in New York. The best physical therapists in the city were down the street from her. She could receive in-home care; I could work. She would heal; we would not kill each other. I would fix her insurance situation and get her back on Medicare and have a private handyman install grab bars in both bathrooms, in the shower and the tub. I would visit her twice a week to manage the caregiver who would fall into our laps as if by magic and whom I would pay out of pocket. That caregiver would be Dora: from the time she set foot in her apartment, my mother hated her.

On this day, my mother, still in a wheelchair, a round brush and Vuitton makeup bag in her lap, has blow-dried her own

hair and applied her lipstick. She has wheeled herself into the
den, where she is ensconced on the sofa, dressed in her leopard
print fleece pants and a Boston University football jersey, her
two atrophied legs outstretched in front of her on the Lucite
and patent leather desk chair where I once wrote term papers
on Charlotte Brontë's fiction and its impact on nineteenth-
century feminist theology during my holidays from college.
Enormous hammered gold earrings through which one might
shoot a basketball graze her shoulders. The television is on;
Perry Mason. My mother has spent all of her money on makeup,
and has been living on nothing; she presents well. We await the
arrival of a community Medicaid examiner. My mother leans
back against a black velvet pillow embroidered in fraying gold
script with the words *You can never have too much luxury.*

Between the hours of nine and eleven, with Dora hovering
over her, my mother will be visited by representatives of a sub-
sidized prescription drug plan; a physical therapist sent by the
office of the orthopedic surgeon who repaired her ankle; a
healthcare consultant who will help us navigate the waters of
the community Medicaid application, since my mother's co-
pays will bankrupt her in a month; three different visiting
nurses; and a divisional case manager, a tall, unsmiling woman
named Tenzin.

"You're all here to see *me!*" my mother says. She gazes wide-
eyed from one person to the next. She laughs and claps her
hands like a small child at a birthday party. One person takes
her pulse and another her temperature and another asks how
far she can go using the walker with the tennis balls.

"Dick says I don't really need to use it," she explains to the
visiting nurse, "and I agree with him. He's a very smart man."

"Who's Dick?" the Medicaid consultant whispers to me. "We have her listed as widowed."

"Her man friend," I say. "He thinks she doesn't need a live-in caregiver either. Or the personal alert button that she refuses to wear around her neck."

We step into the hallway and I begin to explain my mother's belief that men, simply by the presence of a particular appendage, always know best. The consultant stops me.

"We see this all the time. The mother's boyfriend, the angry kids. It's hard on everyone."

We step back into the den, where my mother is being given the once-over by Michael, a tall black physical therapist who is almost outrageous in his handsomeness.

"I can get around just fine without the walker," she says to Michael. Her voice has gone up an octave. She's sweet-talking and chirpy, like a schoolgirl.

". . . but I'd do so much better with *you* on my arm," she adds, batting her eyelashes at him. "Do you know you look *just* like Sidney Poitier in *Porgy and Bess?*"

Bile bubbles up into the back of my throat. He doesn't look a thing like Sidney Poitier in *Porgy and Bess,* or Sidney Poitier in anything. The only thing that Michael and Sidney have in common is that they're both handsome men of color.

"Sometimes latent racism comes out with age and trauma," the very white rehab social worker told me, "so don't be concerned if she says something unusual to the staff. These people are used to it."

"*These people?* Maybe you all tell yourselves that to rationalize it," I said.

"They hear it all the time, dear," she shrugged, "so don't be alarmed."

"How could I not be alarmed?"

"Don't worry so much, *really*," the rehab social worker said.

Today, all my mother sees when she looks at Michael is Sidney Poitier, and he is taking complete advantage of her frothing at the mouth over him.

"Can you show us how you walk?" he says. "We'd all love to see—"

Everyone—the pulse taker, the note taker, the temperature taker, the Medicaid consultant, Tenzin—stops what they're doing and watches.

"Mom," I say, "you can't even stand up alone. Now is not the time—"

"It'll be fine," Michael says, smiling at her. "Let's see what your beautiful mother can do."

He moves the folding black lacquered television table away from her. He stands by with the tennis ball walker, just in case.

She beams; she tosses her hair. She loves Michael.

My mother scoots to the end of her sofa and tries to push herself up. She chews on her bottom lip and straightens her spine. She focuses on the television.

"Perry Mason is so handsome—if he just wasn't so *fat*—"

"He doesn't actually exist, Mom—"

"They said he was gay," she says, wistfully.

"Perry Mason wasn't gay. Raymond Burr was gay—"

"I coulda changed him—"

Michael throws his head back and laughs. She tries to push

herself up again. Nothing. Her face begins to flush; I recognize the moment before the explosion.

Fuck shit fucking shit! Help me up, Elissa—

I step in to give her my hand. Michael waves me away and turns to Dora, who is standing in the doorway of the den.

"Does she actually get around without the walker, Dora?" he asks.

"Never—not once," Dora says, laughing. She shakes her head and sighs.

"Thanks *a lot*," my mother growls. "Just remember who is paying you."

"I'm paying her, Mom. She's not working for you. She's working for me."

Dora has arrived as if by magic, as though she has fallen from the heavens; my mother has never asked who she was or where she came from or who was paying her. I scrape together her weekly fee to try to preserve what little my mother has left.

"So what? I did for you," she shouts, "and now you do for me. You don't know what I gave up for you! Go put on some lipstick. I want to speak to these people. I must speak. I must be heard."

Everyone leans in; Michael shuts the television off.

"I am a *walker*. It is what I live for. My daughter—" she nods over to me—*"she don't want me to walk again."*

"Why do you think that?" Michael asks. "If she didn't want you to walk again, none of us would be here."

"She *hates* me—"

I stare at her. I don't correct her.

My mother smirks. The corners of her mouth betray her; they begin to curl.

"She don't want me to walk again. And—"

She gasps. She closes her eyes tightly and puts her hand on her chest.

What, Michael says.

"She hit me."

Everyone looks up at me.

My knees go soft. I lean against the den wall; I can't breathe. The wind has been knocked out of me. On this day, in my mother's den on the Upper West Side, surrounded by a team of people whose goal it is to help my mother—broken, older, frightened—I want to vanish, to disappear, to vaporize. I want to take my mother's coffee cup, the one that's covered with tiny, lovely delicate little hearts, the one she's been sipping tepid water from all morning and that is now crusted around its rim with Red Red Red lipstick, and smash it against the dust-covered Tunturi stationary bicycle standing in the corner, covered with a bedsheet. I storm into the hallway, where Dora is standing, watching her new charge have a meltdown.

"You fall for her games every time," Dora whispers. She links arms with me and walks me into the living room. She sits me down in Gaga's favorite armchair, the place where she spent every night in the seventies when my mother was newly divorced and out dancing at Studio 54 and Plato's until dawn. I feel woozy. My neck is sweaty. Dora dampens a dish towel and hands it to me; I tuck it inside my collar.

"What do you want to do?" Dora whispers.

"I want to go home."

I want to leave, to go home to my wife and my dog and my house in Connecticut, to the life I have made away from her, separate from her; I want to never, ever come back.

The kingdom of my heart.

"You have to learn to laugh," Dora says, rubbing my back. "She's bored and she's scared. She knows exactly how you'll react. It's all fun for her. She likes to make trouble. I bet she gets those happy hormones from treating you like this."

I drink my water. I stand up. We go back into the den. My mother reaches for my hand. I give it to her. She strokes it and kisses it; she holds it to her cheeks, first one, then the other.

"I don't think that's true—that she struck you," Michael says. "Is it? Because it's a very serious charge."

"Of *course* it's not true," my mother laughs. "I love her. I just wanted to see if you were all listening. It was just a little game."

One by one, the consultants leave; Dora shows them out. I fall back into the one comfortable chair in the den. My mother and I glare at each other. Tenzin sits down next to her and listens to her heart. She takes her blood pressure. I notice a thin red cord on her right wrist.

"Very good," she says, typing numbers into her laptop.

"It's always low," I say.

"And how is yours?" Tenzin asks me.

"She's fine," my mother says. "She just needs to lose some weight."

Tenzin looks at us, back and forth; she shakes her head.

"What kind of name is Tenzin anyway," my mother asks. "I love your boots—" she adds, pointing down. "Liss, you should get some boots like that."

They're bright and colorful, wool-legged, laced a long way up to her knees; Tenzin is very tall and very thin.

"I'm Tibetan," Tenzin says, packing up her laptop. "I come from Lhasa."

My mother screws up her face.

"Isn't that where what's his name—I saw him on the street once, coming out of the Mark Hotel—that bald Chinese guy in the red dress who is always giggling—isn't he from Tibet?"

I pray for the Rapture. I pray for a hole in my mother's ancient white broadloom to open and swallow me up. *Please God take me.*

"The Dalai Lama, Mom," I say. "His name is also Tenzin."

I smile weakly at Tenzin, this Tenzin, to let her know that I know. It's a sycophantic gesture, an obsequious peace offering. By showing that I know the name of the leader of the world's Tibetans is Tenzin, the Tenzin standing in front of me won't go home cursing these two privileged Jewish white women, one of them leaning up against a velvet pillow embroidered with a saying about luxury, who will never know the kind of immigrant, exile hell the woman standing in front of her has likely gone through.

"I was walking down Madison Avenue and all these men were milling around outside the Mark with walkie-talkies and this man in the red dress came out. He winked at me."

"The Dalai Lama did not *wink* at you, Mom," I say.

"You *hate* it when men pay attention to me—you just want me to be alone. She wants me to be alone," she shrugs to Tenzin. "She does—"

"I should be going," Tenzin says. "Be well—"

"I'll walk you out," I say.

"I am not finished with you," my mother shouts.

Tenzin and I stand together in silence. I unlock the front

door. The mirrored vertical blinds are drawn; slashes of light betray the dust that veneers the frames standing on the piano. The tennis awards. Her silver loving cup. My mother and I in matching lace outfits on the steps of Caesars Palace in 1970. My mother on the television soundstage in the late fifties, a sweater casually thrown over her shoulder, her eyes gazing ahead, fixed on something in the future, something lovely.

"I am so sorry—please forgive us. We've had a hard morning."

"Do you have children of your own?" Tenzin asks, slipping her arms through her backpack straps. She looks down at me, unsmiling.

"No."

"Your mother is a very beautiful woman," Tenzin says, stepping into the hallway. "And if you're not careful, she will outlive you."

II

She sits beside Laura on the sofa. She simply does what her daughter tells her to, and finds a surprising relief in it. Maybe, she thinks, one could begin dying into this: the ministrations of a grown daughter, the comforts of a room. Here, then, is age. Here are the little consolations, the lamp and the book. Here is the world, increasingly managed by people who are not you; who will do either well or badly; who do not look at you when they pass you in the street.

—MICHAEL CUNNINGHAM, *The Hours*

19

"IT LOOKS SO GOOD ON YOU, BABY," MY FATHER SAYS.

A family party. I am holding an infant, a girl, seven months old. Tousled white-blond curls and gray-green eyes. A squirmer in pink acid-washed Carter jeans with diaper snaps and a tiny cotton T-shirt flecked with orange spots from the strained carrots I've been spooning into her mouth. A wriggling mass of rubbery baby weight and breath that smells like milk. So much energy, everyone jokes, because her mother did high-impact aerobics late into her pregnancy. It takes two people to keep her still for a change.

On this evening in the late nineteen-eighties, I stand the child up in my lap, directly facing me, holding her under her delicate armpits with their soft folds of tender flesh, devoid of muscle or control. Babies are skin draped over form; who knows how they will grow or what they will become. We gaze at each other, unblinking. I smile. She smiles. I laugh. She laughs. Our stare is direct, mutual, intense. She stops moving, stops pulling, frozen, as if all of her energy has been harnessed and funneled into the scrutiny of this person with the masses of oversprayed hair and gigantic shoulders, who is holding her up.

"Hello, you," I whisper.

Maa, she says.

"What," I say. "Tell me—"

Maa—

"Tell me—"

The baby's face changes, like putty pulled in opposite directions. A smile, a frown, a laugh, a furrow, a smile, a shriek. She pulls back from me and grabs my necklace in a dimpled hand: She shoves it into her mouth, this simple gold chain at the end of which hangs Gaga's monogrammed gold locket, the only thing of my grandmother's that my mother passed on to me when Gaga died. I wear it every day. The baby drops it gently and watches it fall into the depths of my sweater. Gaga loved babies; adored them; crossed streets to say hello to them. I inherited this from her.

The baby's eyes are closing. I stand with her and try to lay her down in her Pack 'n Play. The vise grip she has on me—one hand hooked around my neck like a metal hanger on a rod, the other playing with my hair—tightens. She sighs and puts her head on my shoulder. I put her pacifier in her mouth and she takes it and suckles hard and fast, and suddenly she is asleep. It drops to the floor.

"It looks good on you, Liss," my father says. He is sitting at the dining room table with the baby's mother, watching me and drinking a glass of white wine.

He speaks in Talmudic riddles and Zen koans.

It's time, he is saying. *You need to start thinking about this.*

I turn my back so he can't see me cry. His second wife's first grandchild is asleep in my arms.

My grandchild by proxy, he calls her.

. . .

I AM IN MY MIDTWENTIES. I have left my mother and Ben's apartment on the insistence of my doctor, who says that I will die if I stay. I am living in a small one-bedroom walk-up apartment in Chelsea with Julie, a resident at St. Vincent's Hospital. She needed a roommate, like the thousands of New Yorkers of a certain age who will search the classifieds in *The Village Voice* for someone to simply split the rent, share the space, and hope they're not suddenly living with an ax murderer or someone into some unspeakable fetish, the latter of which, this being New York in the eighties, is a strong possibility. Introduced to me by a mutual friend, Julie took the tiny, narrow bedroom with the door, and I the living room. She will come home late every day after a long shift at the hospital, skulk into the bedroom, close the door, and weep.

Julie is built like a cherub, small and muscular and dark, a tangle of contradictions, a devoutly German Catholic, crystal-wearing, Shakti Gawain–spouting, syringe-wielding caregiver

to sick men and women abandoned by their families and lovers
to die alone. Most of Julie's patients are dying of AIDS; when
no one will touch them—this is early on in the plague, and
common humanity has been replaced with fear—it is Julie who
rubs their backs and their feet and holds them when they cry
like panicked babies, from the innermost depths of their broken bodies. She leaves the hospital exhausted, stinking of dis-
infectant, orange betadine caked around her nailbeds. She
meditates and chants and lights incense; she cleanses with
high colonics and wears a watermelon tourmaline pendant to
ward off evil spirits along with her tiny gold confirmation cross.
She loves sex and fucks anything that moves, anything but me,
whether I am home or not: in cars parked on Chelsea side
streets, in the restroom at her favorite yoga studio on Thir-
teenth Street, in the bedroom we will share in the coming
months. She returns home from the hospital every night, death
on her hands and clothes; she stands in the kitchen, pours
cheap Chardonnay into a heavy Mexican blue-lipped goblet
and tells me a joke that has been traveling the hallways of the
hospital, started by an asshole in the ortho department: *What's
the best diet for someone with AIDS? Flapjacks and flounders.
Flapjacks and flounders? Anything that will slide under the door.*

She laughs. Her knees go out from under her. She is tired.
I hug her. She sobs in my arms.

I am in love with Julie in a way that I have never been in
love with anyone, and we will, in a year, find our way into bed
together. But for now I am sleeping with a man, following the
rulebook as though it will propel me into a life of the predictable and the safe: the husband and the child. The mundane

and the expected. The chance to make things right, to build my own life, to be a different kind of mother. To break what Julie calls the Crazy Chain.

We had been ill with a stomach flu. High fevers. We couldn't make it down the stairs of our apartment building. My mother brought over tubs of chicken soup and rye bread and containers of boiled white rice from a deli. Ben double-parked outside. My mother rang the buzzer.

I'm leaving it on the third-floor landing, she yelled into the intercom microphone. *I don't want to see her. And you're sick. Now buzz me in.*

Julie was competition; the other woman. She was an enemy, charming and beautiful and compassionate, someone entrusted with the care of others who would steal my mother's spotlight, an attention thief whom I was now completely and utterly focused on like a heat-seeking missile. *The Crazy Chain,* Julie said, *had to be broken.* Distance would need to be imposed. My life would depend upon it. But self-imposed detachment from my mother made me feel queasy and hungover and guilty, like a drunk with DTs. When I stopped calling her, my hands shook, and she began showing up at my job. When I hid, she called Julie's pager. When she pronounced me ungrateful and a loser—*You don't know what I gave up for you; how dare you ignore me*—I listened closely, in silence, to her litany of words, their choice and pitch and timbre. I stayed on the phone and wept and believed that she was right.

. . .

RICHARD IS KIND AND BEARDED and gentle, a jazz guitarist moonlighting as a vegetable salesman at Dean & DeLuca in SoHo, where I am working twelve-hour days as the book department manager. He hums Coltrane, he knows the difference between a San Marzano tomato and an Early Boy. He's moved all the way to New York from Bend, Oregon, where his single mother, a devout Mormon, still lives. There's another man on the other side of the store, Oren, an actor moonlighting as a cheesemonger, sweet and long-haired, half Italian, half Jewish, hooded eyes, small round wire-rimmed glasses, a cross between Wings-era Paul McCartney and Armand Assante.

The vegetable man doesn't talk much. He asks me out for a beer one night after work; I go. Three days later, we are in his bed in Brooklyn. We move together like a cymbal-playing windup monkey; sex is mechanical, a purely hormonal explosion between two people not yet thirty. Prime baby-making time for both of us. I come hard, violently, whenever he touches me, wherever he touches me, from the back of my neck to my knees. We barely speak. We have nothing in common and nothing to say to each other, but we do it everywhere we can: in the walk-in after hours, on the foldout futon in my apartment while Julie is on a shift, at midnight on the black linoleum floor of Manhattan Fruitier in the East Village, surrounded by shrink-wrapped holiday gift baskets and a massive gray-striped mouser who stares at me while the vegetable man's head is between my legs. I close my eyes; I see Julie.

"Shouldn't you be married and having babies around now?" my six-year-old cousin Russ announces during Thanksgiving dinner with my father's family. "Shouldn't you be a mommy soon?"

Even at six, he knows the drill. He knows what's supposed to happen, what's expected. The table gets quiet; Aunt Sylvia, my father's older sister, the family matriarch not given to easy approval, is an arbiter of tradition, her tall, teased hair coiffed and sprayed into a foot-high caramel mousse, dressed in a blue-and-gold paisley silk dress. She repeats her grandson's question. *Shouldn't you?* Everyone looks over at me.

It is 1988; a time of excess. Hair is huge, massive shoulder pads make svelte women look like Dick Butkus, drugs are everywhere and easily procured. After we close the store, my friends go out dancing at the China Club or Au Bar. They make out on the catwalk over the dance floor at the Limelight. The vegetable man and I drink longneck Bud Lights at the local Italian dive bar on Mulberry Street and ride the subway back to his place. We fuck for hours on his bare mattress on the floor, a candle stuck in an empty Chianti bottle. Tal Farlow plays on his stereo. We lie on our backs and share a joint. We drink a magnum of screw-top Mountain Rhine that makes my teeth ache. I ride the train back to my apartment alone. The next morning, I don't recall how I got home: the train ride, the Chianti, the jazz, the joint. When I wake up, Julie has left for the hospital. A note written in her doctor's scrawl sits on the dining room table, leaning up against a half-empty bottle of Corona. *Your mother called three times, looking for you. Didn't know what to say. May come to the store later.*

Unlike the vegetable man, Oren the cheese man, who never stops talking, looks at me and my knees quaver; our relationship is heavy flirtation in the locked basement stockroom we call *the cage* and cheap burgers after work. I don't want to be alone with him; I can barely form words when I'm around him. When I see Oren, across the display cabinet housing the smoked fish and the white Italian truffles, my ears burn. Heat floats off my face in sheets.

One night after I close out the register and lock the doors, I meet him at the Old Town Bar, where he is waiting for me, drinking stout from the bottle and watching the Knicks. He sees me in the massive mirror hanging behind the bottles of liquor, turns around, snakes his arm around my waist, and pulls me in to him. He smells rank, of ripe Époisses and olive brine, and I lean hard against him, as though I want him to take on the full weight of me, of my life. Oren and I drink English beer and Manhattans, sharing a bench in a quiet booth at the back of the bar. We eat fatty, wet burgers that drip melted cheese down our chins. We talk about music and food and Sting and Trudy Styler, and what a modern family can look like—men with men, women with men, longtime unmarried couples having babies—and the childbirth scene in *Dream of the Blue Turtles,* which, he admits, made him cry. We make out on the corner of Eighteenth and Broadway, my back pressed against the window of a sporting goods store, cars honking around us. *Get a room.* Oren flags down a taxi and kisses me and helps me in. I drive away, across town and back to Julie, who is dating an accountant; when I get home, I see that she's left her Birkenstocks outside the bedroom door. It rattles in its frame for twenty minutes.

I feed the cats. I sit down at the dining room table and go through the mail. I pour myself a glass of wine, and then another. I try not to listen. I play the messages on our answering machine: *It's your mother. Call me as soon as you get this.* Beep. *I said It's your mother. I demand that you call me. Bye.* The rattling stops. My hands shake; my chest hurts.

The day after my burger date with Oren, a customer wheels a baby into the store. Oren washes his hands and steps out from behind the counter, unbuckles the infant from his harness, and lifts him high into the air. The baby coos with delight. Oren coos with delight. I watch him from my station on the other side of the store, past customers and managers and the whir of a hand-cranked Italian meat slicer. One of the store owners sashays down the aisle with a Pekingese on each arm and says something to me that I don't hear. I steady myself against the counter.

"There's someone I might like," I tell my father that night.

"Have you told your mother about him yet?" he says.

"No," I say, "I haven't."

"Don't," he says. "She doesn't need to know."

We're out to dinner on the Upper East Side: Oren, my father, and his second wife, Shirley. I haven't slept with Oren—excuses: a date with my mother; Julie is at home; our schedules don't mesh—but I'm introducing him to my family. He gets up to use the men's room. My father leans across the table, folds his hands, and smiles. His blue eyes crinkle at the corners.

"We like him," he says, smiling warmly. "Does he like children?"

"He does," I say. "Very much."

"Oh *forgoddsake,* Cy," Shirley says, "stop pushing."

It's okay, I say.

"Babies look good on you," he says. "You didn't tell her yet, did you?"

No, I shake my head. *No.*

I don't want my mother to know, but keeping it from her undoes me; it makes me ill. It feels cruel and spiteful and a vindication for a lifetime of psychic consumption. That a woman's only daughter won't share her joy with her feels wrong. But it will be engulfed, consumed. A partner will force me to choose; a baby will force me to choose. My mother or my child.

After dinner, Oren brings me home to my empty apartment. Julie is away, visiting her family in Nebraska. He leads me into the bedroom and onto the bed and pulls my sweater off over my head. My body is shaking and screaming for him. I close my eyes; I see her.

"Stop—"

He reaches behind me and unsnaps my bra. I feel him against me.

"Really—*stop*—"

What, he whispers.

"I can't—"

Yes, you can—

"No—stop—*I can't*—"

Why? he whispers.

"I can't—*stop*—"

We untangle ourselves. Oren steps into the bathroom. He emerges minutes later. He dresses in silence. He kisses me on the head, like a friend, and leaves.

I see him at the store the next day and the day after that; we avoid each other. We look away.

I want to run, to settle down, to fall in love, to have a baby, but not with him. Not with Oren, or the vegetable man, or any man.

I want to have a baby.

I want to have a baby with her.

. . .

"SO, ARE YOU SEEING ANYONE?" my mother asks. Her eyes are opened wide. She is unsmiling. She stares at my eyebrows while our server scrapes crumbs off our table.

I'm dressed in my SoHo work uniform: pleated black Italian leather pants stuffed into soft, flat boots, an oversized gray sweater, matte makeup, nude lipstick. She and Ben have picked me up in front of the store on Prince Street where I've been waiting for them outside, still in my apron. She rolls the window of the Volvo down and shoos me back inside like she's swatting a fly. Nobody but the help, she says, should be seen in an apron. We drive three blocks west and park around the corner from Raoul's, where we eat at the VIP table in the restaurant kitchen. This irritates my mother, who would rather be in the front room, near the bar.

"I don't even like eating in my *own* kitchen," she says, as the server clears our steaks frites, our tarte Tatin, our coffee. "Don't they know how important you are?"

"I'm one step up from stock girl, Mom—" I say. She winces.

Ben goes outside for a cigarette. She waits for him to leave. She unclips her massive hammered gold hoop earrings and puts them on the table. She has a question for me. *Is there a man.* Because, she says, I seem different.

"No," I tell her. "I'm not seeing anyone."

I drain my glass; a good Côte de Beaune. Our server nods at me and brings another.

"Why don't you go to the Ninety-Second Street Y? Lucille's daughter goes Israeli folk dancing there. She met a fella. Yaron. You could meet a fella."

"I'm not going Israeli folk dancing, Mom—"

"You want to be without a man—"

"I'm *not* going Israeli folk dancing, Mom—"

She wipes her lipstick off on the linen restaurant napkin, hauls out her makeup bag, and dumps it on the table between us.

"So you'd rather be without a man. That's why you have no eyebrows and wear no lipstick. You want to be fat. In an apron. A fat woman in an apron with no eyebrows. Just to spite me. Because you hate me. I know *exactly* who you are. You don't know—"

"—Right—*what you gave up.* Tell me what you gave up," I say. I suck down my wine.

"Men only want women with eyebrows. I know the truth."

"Stop already, forgoddsake—" I say.

"You should be *ashamed* of yourself—" she growls.

"Of what? That I don't look like *you*? That I'm not actually *you*? That I chose not to be? Please, Mother."

She is seething now; almost thirty years of fury bead on her skin like condensation. There is nowhere for it to go; her anger sits on the middle of the table like a bouquet of flowers.

She reapplies her lipstick; she blots her lips with the linen napkin.

"I gave up *everything* for you. I gave up my *life* for you. That you should spite me?"

The server steps over and pours us water. Silence. We stare at each other. Who are we? How did we get to this place of such rage, of such relentless disappointment in each other?

A young French couple come in with an infant and sit down at the table next to us. I force a smile. I'm exhausted. The baby, dressed in a tiny blue-and-white-striped shirt and matching pants, catches my eye. The baby smiles at me. He reaches toward our table and makes a grab for my index finger.

"They like you," my mother says.

"I like *them*," I say, smiling at the child.

"Well, I hope you have a *lot* of money," she says. "Because you know, they cost a *lot* of money."

My mother catches the child's gaze—wearing mounds of shiny, clanging jewelry, she is often the object of baby stares. She sticks her tongue out at it, hard and far and long enough for me to see the muscles in her neck strain and pop. Her face contorts and twists. She's being funny.

The baby lets go of my finger and turns away, confused and unsure.

20

I WAS A SMALL BABY. THE FAMILY STORY: MY MOTHER DIDN'T know she was pregnant for six months. When her fingers swelled and she couldn't get her favorite antique garnet ring off, her sixteen-year-old niece suggested she see a doctor.

In a blurry picture of my parents taken by Gaga in Carl Schurz Park, the evidence is barely noticeable: There is my mother, her blond hair tall and sprayed, the East River a ribbon of musty gray over her shoulder, industrial Queens behind her in the distance. Her wrists are so slender even in her ninth month that her charm bracelet, heavy as Marley's chain, threatens to roll over her knuckles and off her hand. There I am: the incontrovertible affirmation of her pregnancy, and nothing more than a minuscule bump under her pink-and-white cotton blouse. My mother carried me to term, almost nine months from her wedding night. I weighed four pounds at birth, which, for scale, is more or less the size of an average supermarket chicken.

A mother and a daughter are an edge. Edges are ecotones, transitional zones, places of danger or opportunity, says Terry Tempest Williams in her memoir, *When Women Were Birds.* Williams's mother, a Mormon, left her daughter her journals when she died, as Mormon tradition dictates; they were blank. Williams searches for her mother, for her mother's voice, for the edge they shared. *Edges are places of danger or opportunity;* why can't they be both—danger and opportunity? To unpack a maternal disconnect that would result in a mother's not knowing she was pregnant for six months—that she was carrying a life inside her own life—is to court peril. Danger and opportunity coexist in our life, side by side. She carried me. She was pregnant. *An ecotone: a region of transition between two biological communities.* How could she not know that she was carrying another life?

"Because I just didn't," she tells me over breakfast one day, not long before the accident. We're sitting at a diner. I ask her to confirm whether the story is apocryphal, a conjured-up tale by an errant cousin with no particular love for her beloved uncle's new wife.

"But didn't you miss your periods?" I ask.

"Who pays attention to such things?" She shrugs and pulls a silver tube of lipstick and a plastic green compact out of her purse. "I started retaining water. Then I knew there was *a little problem.*"

A little problem: a big deal that will foretell the future. A predictor that she should have paid attention to and perhaps didn't. My father sent her a ten-dollar bill rolled up in a gold pinky ring after running out of cash on their first date. *A little problem with money.* She started retaining water. *A little problem. An unplanned baby.*

My mother pats the space between her rib cage and her navel. She winks. *Retaining water.* She pulls apart a roll. Bits of it fly everywhere.

She peers into the tiny compact, purses her lips, snaps the compact closed, and puts it back in her bag. She stops and lifts a finger to add something; her eyes narrow as though she's trying to focus on something in the distance. A sudden memory, and then a pronouncement.

"I got sick after a while. I started bleeding."

She leans forward across platters of overcooked egg-white omelets, no potatoes, no cheese. The gap between us closes.

"I almost lost the baby," she whispers.

"What?" I say.

"The baby—I almost lost the baby."

"You almost lost *me*?"

"The *baby*," she whispers again, emphatically, peering from side to side. She nods.

"So I had bed rest," she adds. "And then the baby was fine."

She flips open her cell phone and checks her home machine.

My mother speaks of me, prebirth, in the third person, disconnected from her and from the being who grew into the little girl who became the woman sitting opposite her sipping an Americano. *I almost lost The Baby*—the source of her water weight and her sickness, her fat ankles and her swollen fingers. Shame coils around us as we sit in the red Naugahyde booth staring at each other; like cancer, no one dared talk about such things fifty years ago. Women became pregnant, went into the hospital, had babies, and came home. But my mother was as divorced from the workings of her own body, and from who and what she was carrying in her womb, as an amputated limb. Over the years, the disconnect will repeat like a loop: She will have kidney stones and not know it, cystoscopes and colonoscopies without sedation, stitches around her eye without lidocaine, an explosive ankle fracture and want a single white Tylenol. She will carry a growing baby in her belly—another life; a life inside a life, nested like a Matryoshka doll—for six months and not know.

Congenital analgesia: the inability to feel pain, to feel life, to feel joy, to feel death. The ability to will it away, to live a world in suspension. The mother-daughter connection gossamer, flimsy as a crepe.

Like many women of her generation, my mother smoked while she was pregnant: at the six-month mark, after getting the news about her condition, she dieted to excess to retain her pre-pregnancy modeling weight. And then, on a Saturday night at New York Hospital, she gave birth to The Baby, narrow and small, extracted from the birth canal with forceps, the way one might remove stuffing from a turkey.

In keeping with the Jewish custom of naming a child after someone long-lived, they decided that my first name should start with an *E,* for Esther, Gaga's mother, and my middle with an *M,* for my father's grandmother Mary. My father's eldest niece, Maida, had died young, and his family insisted that my *M* should be in honor of her. The first family fight: Would I be named after someone who lived into her late eighties or someone who died in tragedy at fifteen? My mother threatened to walk out. Gaga reminded her of the vagaries of raising a child on her own in the sixties. My mother stayed.

My father was certain I would be a boy; he had chosen Erich, the Germanic spelling. My mother loved Elizabeth, for the queen of England—*It bodes well,* she thought—but was certain that, when asked to spell my name for my nursery school teacher, I wouldn't know how; it would be too hard for me. Eliza wouldn't work, because of Eliza Doolittle. So my mother named me for Elissa Landy, a long-forgotten B-movie actress, and for Mandy Rice-Davies, a model and call girl who figured heavily in the Profumo affair.

You named her after a hooker? Gaga said.

I like it, my mother said.

"So beautiful," my mother says, sipping her coffee at the diner. "The Baby was so small and delicate. Just like a little doll—"

Babies are, by their nature, small and delicate; size and fragility are not exceptional, I tell her.

"But you were," she says. "I used to hold you on one arm, with your head in my palm and your feet nestled in the crook of my elbow. I vacuumed the apartment that way until Gaga yelled at me that I'd drop you."

Did she understand that I was real? That if she dropped me, I would break? Conceivably die? We were one: a life inside a life for nine months. Did her congenital analgesia extend to me?

The words she uses to describe The Baby: spindly, delicate, tiny, petite, dainty, exquisite, fine-boned, wispy. A china doll. Not one to nurse—*I didn't want to risk having a chest like Gaga's*—she feeds The Baby tiny amounts of formula, botching the instructions given to her by the ancient, white-haired obstetrician and Freudian analyst who delivered me, Dr. Heller. The Baby screams all day and all night for the first three months until the next-door neighbor in Yorkville, a German woman with a face like Dietrich and migraines left over from Dresden, tells The Baby's mother that the child is probably hungry: She instructs her to fill The Baby's bottle with thinned-out oatmeal, cut an X in the nipple, and let the child eat. She does, and at last The Baby stops crying.

The Baby also balloons up like a small version of the Michelin Man.

"A giant," my mother says. "Suddenly!"

In an old photograph, The Baby's head, round as a bowling ball, appears to be directly connected to her shoulders, with no involvement of her neck. The Baby's legs are braceleted with cascading bangles of fat, necessitating larger and larger snowsuits and rompers. In home movies, The Baby is plunked down in her playpen on the family terrace and cannot move; she can't get up, or roll over, and doesn't try to crawl, as if the oatmeal weight anchored her to the earth like a yard dog staked to the ground. In one snapshot, The Baby's mother looks exhausted and sad. She hoists her daughter in the direction of the camera.

"I was so ugly and fat afterwards," my mother says when I ask her about the picture. "The Baby, she was the beautiful one. That was what your grandfather said: *Look at her beautiful eyes.* I couldn't stand myself."

In this picture, my mother faces away from the camera, detached, looking at something else. Eventually, the oatmeal weight falls off The Baby and The Baby becomes me.

. . .

"GAGA SAID YOU WERE DAMAGED," my father once told me. "Stood right there at the nursery window at New York Hospital and proclaimed you scarred for life."

I was sixteen; we were eating blueberry pie at the Belmore Cafeteria right after *Taxi Driver* came out. My father's business had failed; my mother had asked him to leave. He had considered, for a moment, *driving a hack.* He was doing research, he said.

A damage; a twin.

I touch my right hand to my temple when he says this. I feel for imperfection, for brokenness. There's a shallow indentation indiscernible to anyone else, a persistent ancient pain that I live with every day. When I was eight, I fractured my skull in a bicycle accident that nearly killed me. On a sunny May afternoon in 1971, I rode my bicycle around our Forest Hills cul-de-sac and followed my friend Todd down a long steep hill that emptied into the exit of an underground parking garage. It was a risky prospect, and not something we were prone to do as mostly thoughtful and obedient children; we could easily have been hit head-on by an oncoming car.

I blacked out somewhere on the way down the hill and careened directly into the concrete wall at the bottom. My brain slammed hard into bone, nearly killing me without a scratch. I regained consciousness at Todd's mother's kitchen table with a cold rag wrapped around my head, a brown stoneware plate of gingerbread cookies in front of me. For a moment, I step out of myself—I see myself sitting at the tiny table in navy blue sailor pants with a fresh hole at the knee the size of a dime; I see the red-and-white-striped T-shirt, and the pink rag around my head dripping down my neck—and there is Liz, Todd's mother, heavy and blond, dressed in a paisley housecoat, on the phone, hands shaking, dialing the rotary, frantically trying to reach my mother. *Where is she? Why can't they find her?* Minutes—hours?—later I am carried through the lobby by Buck, our neighbor, a local boys' school teacher and my father's best friend, out to his white Falcon. I see my mother over Buck's shoulder; our eyes lock and she looks away, her face twisted in terror. I sit on Buck's lap, next to my mother, at our local emergency room. Buck is drenched in cheap aftershave and wearing glen plaid trousers, brown and gold and white. The pattern dizzies me and I pass out, my forehead landing square in the middle of his muscular left thigh. I come to, just as a teenager with a slice running the length of her forearm is rushed passed us, her bone-white wrist peeking out of a blood-drenched flowered kitchen towel held aloft by her mother.

More than forty years later, the dull ache at my temple throbs; it still hurts to the touch. I warn my hair stylist and colorist about it every time.

Remember the spot, I tell them. *Please don't go near it.*

———

"The Baby's here," my mother says to someone, I don't know who, when I come home for a weekend from college; it is her birthday, my freshman year and the first time I have been away from her for any length of time. I walk into her apartment to find her in the kitchen, the telephone receiver nuzzled against her neck, a Tiffany goblet of Soave in her hand.

"She looks terrific—The Baby looks terrific—She lost so much weight—"

My mother hangs up and grabs me in a tight, delicious hug; we don't let go. She kisses the side of my head, quick and hard, over and over, like a woodpecker on a tree; my pain doesn't exist for her. She leaves a hot pink brand in the shape of wax Halloween lips on my temple at my hairline, on what she has called since my accident *the sore spot*.

"I kiss The Baby's sore spot," she says, affectionately. "I kiss it. Kiss. *Kiss*."

21

DORA HAS REARRANGED MY MOTHER'S LINEN CLOSET. AFTER living with her for seven months, my mother refuses to let her caregiver do anything else.

On the middle shelf, my mother keeps a white-and-blue tartan baby blanket folded neatly in thirds and shelved directly at eye level. It is the one that she and Gaga tucked up around me in my metal stroller on cool fall and spring days in the early sixties, once the weather began to turn.

I conflate the sight of the blanket, its rough, oily British wool grazing my tiny infant neck and point of my chin, my small hands buried deep beneath it, with the antique clouds of tuberose and musk clinging to my grandmother's wrists as she forced the fabric around me. The blanket is safety and it is love, and in the split second between sight and memory—my eyes and my heart; the present and the past converge—I open my mother's linen closet door and it tumbles out and lands at my feet in a haze of Manhattan apartment dust. I pick the blanket up and hold it to my face. I inhale. It smells of Gaga, dead thirty-five years. It smells of us.

More than once I have considered liberating it—spiriting the blanket out of the apartment in my overnight bag and bringing it back to my home in Connecticut, where I live the mundane life of a middle-aged adult, in love, laundry to do, errands to run. It would cover me on the couch while I read the Sunday paper, or be spread out on the freezing rocks for a picnic in Maine. I envision it rolled up at the foot of our bed to stave off a chill in the middle of the night, or, having gone threadbare and moth-eaten, draped over my legs on a cold New England afternoon in my later years, when running will be a memory and walking will cease to be easy. The blanket will come home with me and stay, and I wonder where it will end up when I have faded away: at Goodwill, or in a dark green metal clothing dumpster behind the local Congregational church, or swaddled around the grandchild of a distant relative I barely know who, in lieu of the baby I never had, is burdened with the fact of my things.

I stop myself. This was *my* blanket—home movies show me wrapped in it while being pushed in my pram around the Upper East Side of Manhattan—but it is not of me; it belongs to my mother. To take it from the apartment, from her, would be to presume that my past as her baby is severed from our present. To take the blanket from her would be to render me gone, and to imagine that she would neither notice its absence nor miss its memory.

The blanket, this remnant of time and biology, lives there, sandwiched between an assortment of mismatched and tattered fabrics that represent the arc of my life: the worn bedsheets that fit the convertible pullout sofa where I slept for two years in my mother's den, the blue-and-white Scandia duvet cover I used when I was away at college in Boston, a jumble of stiff cotton hand towels with the consistency of sandpaper from my childhood bathroom in Forest Hills. Tucked in among the sheets and towels is a gift box of six heavy cardboard placemats decorated with eighteenth-century sketches of English country parsonages, given to her after a visit by Sally and William, to whom my mother responded with a handwritten note that read *Thank you so much for being Elissa's friend. I appreciate it.*

Other things:

In the entryway coat closet near the kitchen, a tiny red plaid umbrella, given to me by a neighbor when I had my tonsils out at four, hangs next to my mother's mink coat. In the living room closet, old grocery cartons containing my organic chemistry textbooks and Osmond Brothers albums, my collection of Dr. Seuss books and my grade school notebooks are piled up on the floor beneath my mother's shoulder-padded 1980s suits, Yohji Yamamoto skirts, and silver-fox-tipped cashmere shawls. On the top shelf, next to a brown vinyl bag containing a monogrammed bowling ball the color of melting caramel—a present from my father on my twelfth birthday— sits the blue Samsonite train case my mother carried to the hospital when she went into labor with me, a wooden scrapbook stuffed with her publicity clippings, and beside that, a massive silver-and-white-striped cardboard box containing her 1962 wedding gown, involving a monkey jacket and a pillbox hat.

My mother is a keeper of our things, a hoarder of our life together; the sight and fact of them steady and guide her, and when she's having a bad morning, she reviews them, as if taking an inventory of experience. They are proof that we are mother and daughter, that I was once a child utterly dependent upon her. There are my report cards, and my tiny baby teeth stored in a small manila envelope in her jewelry box next to the rosary beads and marked ELISSA TEETH in Gaga's sprawling Palmer Method hand; a lock of strawberry blond hair from my first haircut; the fake pearl ring I bought her for a quarter at an upstate New York hotel gift shop when I was seven; my first-grade notebook, covered in stiff black-and-white cardboard and still stinking of school paste; the wedding gown; the monogrammed bowling ball.

"I spent the morning going through everything," she says when I call to check in on her, to make sure she is up and has eaten and that Dora is there.

"You were such a *darling* baby. But that goddamned bowling ball, Lissie—"

I tell her to get rid of it, just to toss it. She can't, she says.

"It belongs to you. It's *monogrammed!*"

We giggle at this together—a delicious private laugh that comes from a secret shared history belonging only to us—and at the utter absurdity of it: that my father, possessed of a jumbled, inappropriate formality, would force the implied value of inheritance onto the mundane. He thought it would be a good idea to monogram a bowling ball like a piece of fine jewelry, as if it, too, were to become a family heirloom in the manner of the engraved Tiffany pill case I gave to my mother after Ben died, meant to be passed down to the next generation and the one after that in the same breath as a vintage train case, a Kennedy-era wedding dress, an English woolen baby blanket.

22

I AM LYING ON MY BACK ON AN EXAMINATION TABLE. MY FEET are resting in metal stirrups; a lime-green paper sheet is stretched across my lap. It is cold in the room. I'm shivering; my legs tremble.

My father has recently died in a car accident. Susan and I have left her tiny cottage in the Litchfield hills and moved to the ranch house closer to New York, where Susan works every day. We see thirty houses before deciding: a quaint farmhouse on the Hudson, whose resident army of fire ants attacked my ankles as I walked through the overgrown perennial garden. A stucco Tudor with a stream flowing through the basement, owned by an Italian sulky driver who races at a nearby track. A decrepit colonial on a busy street, built around a massive stone fireplace.

The ranch house, for us, is ideal: neither too big nor too small, it is perfect for a couple, perhaps with a child or two. Older parents who will visit us—my mother, Susan's mother—will have no trouble navigating the stairs, because there aren't any. It is in a lovely community filled with farm stands and markets, a short drive from the commuter train, two hours from Manhattan.

The school system, the real estate broker tells us when she shows us the house, *is excellent.*

Susan and I have been together for four years. I have left New York City for good; the tiny apartment in which I have been living since Julie moved to San Francisco ten years earlier has been sold. Connecticut is now my home; Susan is my home. Children enter into our conversation at every turn: over dinner, over drinks, over hikes, over dog walks. We talk about adopting, which, in this early part of the twenty-first century, can still be problematic. We hear stories of people we know—same-sex couples who have been together for years—who plan for adoption organization home visits by hiding evidence of coupledom: pictures are stashed, joint checkbooks and bank statements removed, bills shredded; one-half of the couple moves out. A family cloaked in deception; they are rendered invisible. Having stepped out of one shadow—my mother's—I cannot step back into another one. I make a doctor's appointment. Because I am ten years younger than Susan, I am the obvious one.

Twenty-five years earlier, Susan and her partner, Judy, made a baby with the help of a friend named Charles. Deep into her second trimester, Judy got sick; an infection. Susan slept on the floor of her Manhattan hospital room as her partner, burning with fever, was pumped full of antibiotics. It was a choice: the life of her partner, or the life of her child. Judy lost the baby. They saw it; they said goodbye.

"It had been a little girl," Susan said.

How is grief metabolized? How is it possible to breathe again? They never tried to have another. Their relationship collapsed, perhaps under the weight of the kind of sorrow that infiltrates the cells of the body, that lives on, as the Chinese say it does, in the lungs and the hips. Grief that changes the color of the sky. The prospect of life, of hope, of the cycle that is human existence—mother/child/mother/child—begat death.

We rarely discuss it; the subject is changed.

"You don't have a lot of time," the doctor tells me.

He looks weary and sad; he is squeezed like a sausage into stained blue scrubs, his tan hair brushed into a wiry, unruly comb-over. He appears older than his years; how many lives has he carried into this world? How many lives has he seen lost? How many daughters and mothers?

I am a new patient: He delivered my neighbor's daughters fifteen years earlier at a local hospital near our new home. He came highly recommended when I said that I needed a doctor; I didn't say why.

"You should have started ten years ago," he says.

"Ten years ago I was alone and living in Manhattan," I say.

"So? Single women in Manhattan have babies alone all the time, if they want them badly enough. You would have been thirty, right?"

"Right," I say, staring at the yellowing stains on the chipped acoustic ceiling tiles hanging above me. Someone, years ago, had taped a color Xerox of a mountain lake directly above the table; the tape is peeling, and the picture, ripped.

"Even thirty can be hard for some women," he says, sighing. He pushes himself away from the table and rolls to the other side of the room.

"How old was your mother?"

"Twenty-eight."

"First pregnancy?"

"Only pregnancy," I say, looking at the ceiling. "Except when I was twelve."

. . .

MY MOTHER SPOKE ON THE phone in hushed tones to her few friends living in our building in Forest Hills. A Danish woman, Inga, whose magician husband was prone to roving and who herself had quietly taken a boyfriend of her own, a factory worker she called Hawkins. Melanie, a svelte woman in thick blue-lensed aviators, whose husband, Stan, was not her husband at all, although he was the father of her two children. Vicky, formal, tweed-wearing and cashmere-turtlenecked, whose handsome older son, Don, had filched the bicycle storage room key from one of our inebriated doormen, copied it, and fucked the bored and horny neighborhood women on the dank basement floor amid a tangle of Schwinn wheels and clouds of Clorox.

I hid at the edges and corners of my mother's life. I strained to hear her on the phone every day, listening for clues that I would follow like a trail of crumbs.

"That's what Hawkins likes to do?" my mother laughed on the phone to Inga while I stood just out of eyeshot, tucked behind a kitchen louver door. "Lucky you. I'll call you later."

It is 1975 and my father comes home from work, pours himself two double Scotches, and drinks them in rapid succession. My mother has given up cooking for a job in the city; the act of sustaining is in the past. Every night, we pile into the car and drive to a nearby mall that reeks of patchouli incense and Fryolator oil. We set a time to meet, giving ourselves an hour apart. My father has a cigarette and then another, sitting alone near a fountain that shoots recycled water up into the air and down into an atrium pool. I find the record store, the candle shop, the sporting goods store. My mother tries on clothes at a boutique and buys me a succession of skintight T-shirts with white iron-on block letters that spell out my name. Convening in the atrium, we ride the escalators up to Cookie's Steak House on the top floor and eat our meal in heavy wooden chairs designed to look like small thrones; my mother and I sit in the queens' chairs, my father in the king's. They stare at each other over heavy Hall china plates laden with salad bar chickpeas and Bacos and baskets of crumbling Southern fried chicken.

"I need a small procedure," my mother says, picking at her salad.

A mistake, she says, has been made. *A little problem.*

My father looks away and lights a cigarette.

She goes into the hospital for an overnight. My father stays at a nearby hotel and brings her home the next day. She takes to her bed for a week; the shades are drawn. Gaga comes over to cook. Inga brings her magazines, wedges of low-fat Danish cheese, bottles of Soave.

"Tell me about school," my mother says when I get home and run into her room to make sure she's still there, that she hasn't vaporized while I was in math class, that this all somehow hasn't been a ruse. That she was planning on leaving all along, going back to singing. Walking out, like my grandmother.

She sits propped up against a stack of pillows lined against the wall, overlapping like dominoes. The pillowcases are crisp and ironed by Gaga, as if illness or infirmity can be fended off by tidiness. She is wearing fresh linen pajamas, tailored and striped, a top and a bottom, like a man's; she is made up as though she is about to go out for the evening, surrounded by books and magazines and her makeup bag, the television blaring *The Mike Douglas Show.* A cup of cold coffee is on the nightstand next to her. She looks well, *very well,* I think, and if I asked her to do something she would love to do—Take me shopping? Try out some makeup on my twelve-year-old face? Get up and sing?—I am certain that she would spring out of bed. What has happened to her cannot be seen; she has lost something internal, something vital, a part of herself like her blood type, or the color of her eyes.

She pats the end of the bed for me to sit down next to her. I stare at her. Her vulnerability frightens me.

"Stay with me, honey," she says. "Talk to me."

"I don't know what to do," I say.
"Stay with me—"

"So, there were two pregnancies?" the doctor asks me.
"Yes."
He stands up and opens the door.
"Get dressed and meet me in my office."

. . .

"YOU WILL HAVE FIVE CHILDREN," a medium once told me.

For my birthday in 1988, Julie gave me the gift of a natal chart reading. I sat like a supplicant on a brown leather Moroccan pouf opposite a large triangular woman perched on a dusty batik-covered daybed set a foot off the ground on a dark wooden base. She was pale as snow, the size of a mountain, and topped by a mass of cherry-red hair the consistency of cotton candy. Every surface in the apartment was covered by books or magazines or cats. Between us on a narrow altar she spread out the findings of my reading, based on the information supplied to her: Cancer with Pisces rising. Date of birth. Time of birth. Place of birth. Father's date of birth. Mother's date of birth.

A lover of water, friends, family, babies, music, art. Nurturing. Intensely loyal. Easily distracted. Prone to melancholia. In need of safety and assurance. Security. Guarded. Will hide if threatened. Possessed of a sensitivity disconcerting to others.

Five children.

"Do cats count?" I ask.

"No," she laughs, "they don't. Are you involved with any-one?"

I think of Oren. The vegetable man. Julie.

The medium hauls her girth forward from her seat and traces a line on the chart with the tip of her finger. Her orange polish is chipping, her nails bitten and ragged. She follows the shape of a constellation.

"You will have a tendency toward poor health and excess. You will put someone first. A mother or a child."

"Which?"

"Not clear."

. . .

WHEN JULIE MOVED TO CALIFORNIA to begin her fellowship, I settled into a small, dark, beautiful East Side studio apartment which my mother and I co-owned—I couldn't have afforded it without her help; a Faustian bargain, my friends said—and where I would live for the next decade, until I met Susan. It was a midway point; a rest stop between the past and the fu-ture. My mother, delighted by my moving to the East Side, her favorite part of town, eagerly helped me decorate the space: a massive bookshelf occupied one wall, my Irish pine dresser an-other. Instead of both a couch and a bed, she suggested a sleigh bed that, with the addition of decorative pillows, would func-tion as both; she had seen something like it in *Metropolitan Home*. She generously bought it for me and had it delivered the day I moved in; it was carved and delicate and slender as a tongue depressor, a single bed in which I could comfortably sleep alone.

Once Ben died, our weekends were spent together as a matter of course. We had brunch in silence, sitting opposite each other over platters of bagels and lox at Barney Greengrass or Burgundian omelets at Madame Romaine de Lyon. She liked to go shopping after we ate, and I sat in the man chair, tired and exasperated as a husband, while she took mounds of clothes into the dressing room, stepping out to model them for me, spinning and twirling the way she had for so many years in Ben's fur showroom. After Ben's business shut down, my mother had gotten a job as a secretary to a Fifth Avenue pediatrician a few blocks from my apartment. I often came home to find her waiting for me in the lobby at the end of the day, her arms folded across her chest.

"Why didn't you send her up?" I'd whisper to the doorman. "She has a key."

"She didn't want to invade your privacy," he'd whisper back.

Living in my small apartment with its bed for one, I was quietly involved with both men and women, as though sleeping with the former might mitigate my attraction to the latter. We worked around the problems presented by the furniture. There was a tall midwestern advertising executive who had shoulder-length hair and a collection of ties from the fifties and left me every Saturday morning to play soccer in Central Park. A Long Island commercial real estate guy who looked like Woody Allen, and the lovely man from work who got us both drunk on sake in order to consummate what had been a years-long office flirtation. The Greenwich Village social worker who chained her elderly Bichon to her radiator, just out of reach of her water bowl, to keep her from wandering around her apartment all night and peeing on the loveseat. The CNN newscaster who made love like an angel and forgot to mention her wife.

I would not consider settling down with any of them. I was not single; I was taken. I was married to my mother.

I was her child; I was her spouse.

. . .

"DO YOU KNOW HOW OLD your mother was when she went through menopause?" the new doctor asks me.

Susan is at work in Manhattan, so it is just the two of us in his cluttered office. Pictures of his family are propped up on the credenza behind him: a tall blond wife standing outside her real estate office. Two blond children in soccer uniforms. A golden retriever with a tennis ball in its mouth. Diplomas from Cornell, Chicago, Hopkins.

"I don't," I say.

"You never thought to ask her?"

"We don't have that kind of relationship. Why?"

"Because you're in menopause."

"But I just turned forty-one—I'm still getting my period—"

"I'm seeing women going through it younger and younger. We can start with Clomid injections. We can teach Susan how to give them to you. Are you okay with needles?"

I nod. I shiver. I look down at my hands. My left one instinctively holds my right. The doctor opens his desk drawer and removes a heavy black three-ring binder. Donor listings from a local Connecticut sperm bank.

"What are the side effects?" I ask.

When I lived in Manhattan, I saw scores of women in their late thirties marching up Park Avenue pushing multiples in Italian strollers that cost as much as a Volkswagen. Clomid babies, I called them.

"Do twins run in your family?" the doctor says.

23

MY FATHER, WHO HAD FLOWN PLANES OFF A MOVING AIRCRAFT carrier at night in the Pacific during World War II, was running an errand two miles from his Long Island home on a sunny August morning. He was broadsided by a bunch of teenagers in an uninsured, speeding Honda, with his second wife, Shirley, sitting next to him. She, with lesser but still severe injuries, was taken to one hospital, he to another. After twenty years during which they were inseparable—they saw each other through surgeries and the loss of parents, the illness of Shirley's son and the birth of her grandchildren, job changes and retirements, house moves and my father's depression that flowed through their lives like a slow stream—she would never see him again.

This is the work of the living, of the child for the parent, the partner for the partner. These are the things that are done; the unextraordinary. I planned my father's funeral while he was still alive; It was decided when and under what circumstances I would end his life support. I wrote the obituary and filed it with the paper; a flag for his casket was secured from the Veterans Administration. I thought of things for him to take, as though he were going on a journey: the rubber pocket comb that he was never without, a picture that he carried in his wallet of us together in New Hampshire, a linen handkerchief, his Navy wings, the gold heart charm that he had made for my mother in their earliest days—CY LOVES RITA engraved on its back—and that he begged her to give me after the divorce, which she did. I conspired to arrange these things around him in his simple wooden kosher casket the way an Egyptian pharaoh might be surrounded with necessities for the afterlife, tucked beneath the traditional shroud that he was buried in; it would have been forbidden. Grieving in the Jewish tradition lasts for a year; those left behind say the Mourner's Kaddish every morning. Beyond that, Jewish death is a journey of simplicity, of light travel, of dust to dust. No matter how beautiful we are, how wealthy, how tortured, how loved: we come with nothing; we leave with nothing.

· · ·

"WAS THERE *ANYTHING*—" MY MOTHER began to ask when I told her that her ex-husband was gone. She stopped herself.

I couldn't speak; I didn't answer.

"He's gone, Ma—" I said, finally.

For a month after my father's death, my mother gave me a wide berth: Instead of three calls a day, there was just one. *Are you okay? You have to remember to eat. Don't drink too much. Get your highlights done. You'll feel better. Do you need some things? Call me back. You're making me nervous.*

She did not expect me to drive to Manhattan to see her for dinner more than once a week. Her proximity to her ex-husband's affairs of the dead felt precarious. The boundaries of my grief frightened her. I had been my father's only child in the way I am my mother's: It had been my responsibility to sit with him in the last comatose, morphine-addled week of his life, to make sure his needs were tended to, to bury him, to finalize his life, in the way I would someday have to do for her. But at night, when I awoke in bed at three and four, the tentacles of sorrow squeezed the air out of my lungs; they wrapped themselves around me and splintered my rib cage like chicken bone. Out of a deep sleep, they forced me to the floor of our house in a heap, where I sobbed and heaved in breathy gasps until Susan brought me back to bed.

There was a jungle of sorrow that I crawled through, hand over hand, that tripped me when I least expected it—in my sleep, going for a walk, making dinner, making love—and left me blind with an unpredictable kind of mourning that terrified my mother.

"You just need a new look," she said. "I'll meet you at the salon."

I went, and she sat in the chair next to me, scanning my face in the mirror, begging me to smile.

Please, honey; please. Just once. You have such a pretty face. Let's do a makeover.

She could not comprehend my grief; it was alien to her. My hard-won relationship with my father enraged her. Even dead, the fact of him incensed her; when his name was on my breath, she was not at the center of my world. She had always believed that I had chosen him over her. Our little family was simply a competition that he had won.

In the weeks after he died, in the silence and space that my mother allowed me, I spent endless days at my desk, staring out at our garden. My father consumed my work—his life, death, the fact of depression and grief and how they can be inseparable—took over my days and obscured them. I considered what it meant to be an adult daughter, an only child who, late in the life of one parent, becomes that parent's friend. And what does it mean for that parent to become a friend to his now-middle-aged daughter. Our relationship had shape-shifted over the course of our forty years together: He had grown kinder and softer with time and the love and steadiness that he found in the last third of his life. I unclipped the anger that I carried for him as if it were a torn, useless rigging, and I let it blow away. It was no longer relevant. I no longer needed it; I replaced it, somehow, with love.

If it had been possible with him, I thought, it could be possible with her too.

. . .

A MONTH TO THE DAY after his death, after the papers were filed
and the insurance claims made and I began the work of living
the rest of my life without him, my mother had had enough. A
month was all she could take.

The phone rang in my office at dusk. It was hot out; Susan
and I were sitting on the deck, facing the garden, drinking a
strong concoction of fresh-squeezed lime juice and two shots of
dark rum stirred together with palm sugar, invented by my
friend Sally's husband, William, who in the late seventies put
himself through school by tending bar. Susan made them in
massive Italian highball glasses, and we sipped them gingerly.
They were deadly, and drew bees.

The edge in my mother's voice caught and then stopped,
like a serrated knife. It was a familiar sound, one that was as
recognizable as my own face in the mirror.

"Elissa," she said that night on the phone.

Elissa.

The small window air conditioner blew gusts of wet, cold
air at my face while I stared out at the garden, the phone
cradled against my shoulder. The room was decorated in
Depression-era pictures of Susan's family in rural Connecticut,
all of them women.

"It has been a month since he died," my mother said. "And
now it's time for you to focus on me."

The sliver of time between stimulus and reaction.

"Mom, I have a question for you—" I said.

"Yes—" she said.

"I was at the doctor. He wants to know—when did you go through menopause?"

"What the hell kind of question is that! Are you thinking about having a *baby*—?"

"I'm just asking—" I said.

"You'll be fat as a house," she said. "Who's gonna pay for it? *You?*"

"When, Mom—I just need to know."

"I was done at thirty-nine," she said.

Thirty-nine?

"You never thought to tell me?"

"It never seemed important," she said.

I put the phone down on my office chair; I could still hear her voice. I walked away, down the hallway, through the kitchen.

I went out onto the deck, past Susan sitting in an Adirondack chair reading, the dog at her feet. I walked across the yard and into the bursting vegetable garden. We had no money that year, and every meal we ate came from the earth and was composted back to the earth. I sat down at the edge of a box, the one in which we had planted spinach, chard, masses of kale growing on thick stalks. I raked my fingers through the damp soil until heavy lines of it lodged under my nails in black stripes. I forgot the lone screw at the corner of the box, which had come through the wood when we built the garden. I caught the back of my hand against it, scraping it hard. A ribbon of red snaked between my pinky and ring finger and into my palm.

I felt nothing; I watched the blood drip into my hand as though it belonged to someone else.

24

EVEN NOW, THIRTY-SIX YEARS AFTER HER DEATH, THE ESSENCE of Gaga hangs in the bowels of my mother's living room closet, among her silver-fox-tipped cashmere shawls and her mink reefer coat, her Norma Kamali jackets and Ben's Armani tuxedo with the crisp round cigarette burns on the cuff from a wild party at the Friars Club. In the darkness behind the foil-and-peach-wallpapered sliding doors, Gaga is there, her Jungle Gardenia and Youth Dew suspended in a cloud of the Aqua Net that she sprayed and sprayed, shellacking herself inside a carapace.

When Gaga died, during a freak spring snowstorm when I was a freshman in college, my mother got rid of most of her things, parceling them out to friends and neighbors. A dressing table went to the granddaughter of a friend who liked to play dress-up. Her ornate marble-topped coffee table went to the niece of my mother's friend Olga in New Jersey. My mother kept the Persian lamb coat her mother had rarely worn, and the purse she was carrying at the time of her death; she kept a few pieces of her jewelry and, on a small end table in my mother's bedroom, Gaga's dressing set that she'd been given when she turned sixteen: a horsehair brush, a yellow Bakelite comb, and the long-handled mother-of-pearl makeup mirror in which my mother still applies her lipstick every morning, over and over, as if Gaga can see her from the other side. As if she can tell exactly how beautiful her daughter has turned out, against all odds.

The ghosts of lost family members with unfinished business make their presence known this way, and when my mother sent me back to the apartment to pick up clothes after she went into rehab, I inhaled the combination of flower and earth and aerosol particulate that my grandmother had become, living like a phantom amid the stuff of our lives. Although I am not dead, my own ghosts are in there alongside hers, in my locked brown tweed college suitcases that haven't been opened in thirty-five years, in the Associated Grocery cartons of my child-hood that my mother dragged into the city when she married Ben, packed with ancient textbooks and bags of Kodak Insta-matic photos, the athletic awards for the feats that made me popular for a few delicious seconds after they happened. But everywhere, wrapped around us like a shroud, is Gaga. And when I push open the closet door to look for the clothes to bring to my mother in the rehab where she would spend forty-one days and nights after her accident, I am overcome.

. . .

THE CLOSET HAS OVER THE years become a time capsule, a por-
tal, an architectural dig site. On the top shelf of the closet sits
the disintegrating, carved-wood 1950s publicity scrapbook that
Gaga assembled when my mother was on television before I
was born. When I was very young and my parents went out for
dinner on a Saturday night, I sat next to Gaga on the couch and
we read my mother's publicity clippings aloud together, like a
children's story; she was teaching me to read. RITA ELICE'S CO-
PACABANA DEBUT; RITA ELICE WINS SILVER LOVING CUP ON WPIX
COMPETITION; CHOLLY KNICKERBOCKER SAYS *FOLLOW THAT GIRL!*

Never forget that this is your mother, Gaga would say, carefully turning the heavy black scrapbook pages one by one. *She
was once very famous, a long time ago.*

I consider packing up my mother's scrapbook that Gaga
had so lovingly assembled and bringing it with me to rehab; I
decide that it is too fragile, that if it is lost or damaged, it will
be irreplaceable for her. On the shelf beneath the book is the
white-and-silver garment box that holds my mother's ivory lace
wedding gown and pillbox headpiece.

It's a Givenchy style, Gaga would say when I was a child,
*and you will wear it down the aisle when you get married. She's
saving it for you.*

In my mother's wedding photos, she towers over my father
by more than six inches; for years, I try to envision myself wearing the dress—masses of ivory Dupioni silk hemmed up to accommodate the massive difference in our heights, the pillbox
bobby-pinned to the top of my head, my face obscured by a full

veil as required by Jewish law. My mother's wedding dress is a family talisman, a guarantor of life and future, of more children and the continuation of our family and our bloodline, mother to daughter.

Collecting my mother's requested items to bring back to rehab, I stand on her old wooden ladder and nudge the dusty lid off the garment box; I reach in for my mother's wedding dress, to feel the fabric and touch the person she once was, before I was born. The box is empty.

. . .

BY THE TIME I KNEW her, Gaga was no longer an attractive woman. Her white-blond hair had never once been colored, and with age it had gone directly from the strawberry blond of her childhood and middle years to platinum when she turned fifty. Since the early 1930s, she had combed it straight back and rolled it into a tight French twist bobby-pinned and shellacked into place with hairspray, rendering it immobile even in the most ferocious of storms. Broad and boxy, she was stout and shaped like an old-fashioned round-edged Frigidaire, with a heavy sagging bosom and belly that she secured with a massive girdle that closed with twenty hooks and eyes. Twenty, I know, because one day when I was ten, she called and asked me to go down to the newsstand on the corner and get her a paper. I let myself into her apartment while she was in the bath, found the girdle on her bed, and counted them, hook by

hook. The piece was massive, old-fashioned, with bone sup-
ports that ran the entire length of it, like armor.

Turn around, Elissa—don't look, she said, stepping out of
the bathroom in her yellow chenille robe. I faced the window
and the Long Island Railroad tracks outside until I heard the
robe drop to the other bed, then sneaked a glimpse over my
shoulder. Gaga gazed at the floor, the girdle around her waist
inside out and inverted so that the bra portion hung down to
her knees. She hooked all twenty eyes, turned the girdle
around, and slipped her massive, pendulous breasts into it. I
looked back out the window, but not quickly enough.

"You *saw*," she said, her voice angry and low.

"I'm sorry, Gaga—I didn't see," I said, still facing the window, my back to her.

"You don't need to see such an ugly body, Elissala," she
said. "This is what old looks like. Old is not pretty. Old should
be dead. Pushing up daisies, Mamale."

"Don't say that—"

My words choked me.

"Well, what do you think? That I'll live forever?"

· · ·

I SEARCHED THE CLOSET FOR the clothes that my mother requested. I pushed and pulled hangers to see what I could find
but came up with nothing except a silk crepe dressing gown
that had been shoved all the way in the back, its belt creased

and snaked through low loops so that its owner could tie it around her hips; mauve and dusty blue, it was meant for a tall, thin woman from another era.

"It's Gaga's," my mother said when I called her to describe it. "From her flapper days, when she was still beautiful. Lay it across your face and breathe. It's like she's still here."

25

I WANT TO KNOW.

I want to understand.

No family likes having a writer in their midst, says a close friend. With eleven books to her name, she knows this. No family ever says *Yay. A writer.*

My office is piled high with journals that follow me through childhood—the earliest is dated 1976, when I was thirteen— into high school, college, the years I was living with Julie. The last entries are dated in the nineties, when I knew that it was time for me to leave New York, and that in my simply knowing this, simply *understanding* it, I was reclaiming my own life. My journal entries all ask the same question: *Who is she?* Where did her mania come from? Why the paranoia, the jealousy, the temper tantrums? Why the beauty that itself was so furious, a painting created in fear, like *Starry Night,* whose wild brush-strokes are a direct translation of the churning mind that created them? I want to know what happened to her, and in doing so, what happened to us. *What had I done wrong? What could I have done differently?*

If I can understand her, I can love her better, while there is still time.

These are the last years; I want to change our story.

. . .

"HOW ARE THINGS TODAY?" I ask Dora.

She looks lovely, this petite woman in her forties, this caregiver for other people's older parents. This is the new tribe, the new potlatch: We pay strangers to care for the people who raised us—shitty job or not—at the end of their days, and every day becomes a ceremony of routine. The joyous coffee; the wonderful book; the favorite movie.

"She's good—we did her exercises this morning, Miss Elissa."

"Did she eat?"

Dora laughs and rolls her eyes.

"She's refusing again."

"Did she say why?"

"Because she says she ate yesterday. That's what she does:

gorges one day and starves herself the next. She says she doesn't want to be *homely*."

"Homely? She used that word?"

Antiquated verbiage, a remnant from another time, an ancient bit of vocabulary, meaning two separate, conflicting ideas: *comfortable, relaxing* and *ugly, unattractive*.

Dora shakes her head and laughs.

"Your Mama could never be homely. She would never let it happen. She got more makeup in the mail yesterday. She said it was Mother's Day and she was buying herself a present. I said, *But it's not Mother's Day, Mrs. H.,* and she said, *Every day is Mother's Day for me.*"

"*I hear you talking about me!*" my mother shouts from her bedroom.

"I'll leave you two alone," Dora says, walking me down the hallway.

My mother is propped up in bed, in her leopard print robe and full makeup. The television is on. She's watching *Casablanca* for the tenth time this month. She pats the duvet cover.

"Sit with me," she says. "Come, honey. You look beautiful. Let me see what you're wearing."

I freeze.

I gaze at the mirrors that line her bedroom walls.

Slim jeans. Suede winter boots. An oversized navy blue turtleneck sweater. Before my mother's accident, I wore contact lenses; she hated my glasses. But now I'm wearing tortoiseshell frames. Big tortoiseshell frames that are, I realize, smaller versions of hers.

"You look terrific, sweetheart—"

"What's the catch, Ma?" I say.

Instinct: deflect, fight, flight.

"Already you're starting with me? You just *got* here—"

She laughs and pats the middle of the bed, the demilitarized zone between her side and Ben's.

"Come, honey," she says. "Sit with me."

My mother's side of the bed, near the window and the bathroom, has collapsed with time. It sags a good four inches below Ben's side, which is piled high with music, the *Times,* old bank statements seven years old, flowered makeup bags overflowing with samples.

I can hear Dora in the den, talking on her cell phone to her husband in Jamaica.

"Do you need me, Mrs. H.?" she yells.

"*I don't need her!*" my mother shouts back. "Like a hole in the head I need her. She eats my food."

"She doesn't eat your food, Mom—she has her own food. She's living here. She has to eat *something.*"

"I found a chicken leg missing. She twisted it off the roaster I ordered from Fine and Shapiro. Just tore it right off, like a handle."

"Maybe you ate it during the night?"

"Are you calling me *a liar?* You always take her side—"

"Okay, Mom—" I say. "Stop. You need her."

"I don't need her."

"*I* need her," I say. "I sleep at night because of her. How would you cook for yourself? How would you bathe? How would you get back and forth to physical therapy?"

"How's the dog?" she asks.

"You *do* need her—Jesus, Mom—there's no air in here."

I look around. The windows are sealed with thirty years of city dirt. The radiator is pumping hot, dry air into every room in the apartment; plants die here the moment they arrive. The ficus tree she and Ben once bought at a street fair on Columbus Avenue instantly wilted in the living room. She decided it needed more sun, so she lashed it with a shoelace to the terrace fencing, where it eventually blew away, across West End Avenue and into the Hudson River.

Standing in my coat, I'm starting to sweat. I pull at my turtleneck; my neck is damp.

"I'd get along without her very well—" my mother says.

She throws her head back, like she's onstage; she begins to sing.

I get along without you very well
Of course I do
Except when soft rains fall
And drip from leaves that I recall
The thrill of being sheltered in your arms

"You sound good, Ma—"

"Stay with me, sweetheart. Come sit—" she says, patting the bed.

I bring a stack of magazines over to her.

She reaches up to me. I bend down. Her arms are like twigs that could snap in the hands of a child. She wraps them around me, barely making it the width of my shoulders. She strokes the back of my neck. I'm distant, careful. She feels my reticence. How could she not.

"I can't stay," I tell her.

"Of course you can't," she says, pulling away from me. She looks out the window.

"Take your coat off. Let me make you something—"

"I ate already, Mom—"

"An egg—"

"I don't want an egg—"

"You should eat an egg. All protein—"

She reaches over and touches my stomach.

"Can I get you a coffee?" I say. "I'll run over to Starbucks."

"Sit—" she says. "*Talk to me*. Tell me what's going on."

I think about what to say.

She opens *Vogue* and flips through it, page by page.

. . .

"DO YOU REMEMBER THE VERUSCHKA article, honey?" my mother says, tossing the magazine off the bed into a basket filled with other magazines. She picks up *Harper's Bazaar* next.

"Of course I remember," I tell her. Even as a child, I found Veruschka oddly compelling. In the images, she reclines languidly; her gaze is soft, her right hand to her temple in ennui or sadness, a white porcelain cup of tea—it must be tea; she is hurtling through Japan in a first-class carriage on the Shin To-kai-do in this 1966 Richard Avedon fantasy—resting near her elbow. Wearing a short pale mink jacket casually tossed over brocade sashes and voluminous, flowing knickers, Veruschka is the quintessence of effortless grace, texture, and wistful longing.

The Veruschka article, torn out of a 1966 issue of *Vogue*, sat on our entryway table, on our breakfast counter, in my parents' bedroom. I was three years old when the twenty-six-page story appeared in the magazine. "The Great Fur Caravan," starring Veruschka, was a talisman, a reminder, a beacon of hope and possibility for my mother, who had stepped off the runway, out of the Stork Club, and away from the television stage in order to raise me and be the wife she was expected to be by my advertising executive father. The greater the distance from who she had once been, the more obsessed with Veruschka she became, studying her as though cramming for a test; the easy posture, the sulky splendor, the lyricism, and the coats, the capes, the skirts, the mittens of fox, chinchilla, mink, and lynx that she herself would have modeled before her marriage and motherhood, and the mere thought of which transported her back to the safety and elegance of her former life, if only for a few minutes.

Stuck in suburban Queens, my mother funneled every ounce of unwavering energy into fashion and beauty and fur; by 1970, she had amassed four fur coats and assorted hats, muffs, and wraps—fox, mink, ocelot, and nutria filled her closet, as though she herself was embodying the Great Fur Caravan—and taught my seven-year-old tomboy self to identify them, a test she would repeat through the years so that I could tell the difference between a sable and a mink when I grew up.

Years later, as a teenager, I feigned interest if only for the attention; my mother misinterpreted it as curiosity, and while my own first fur wouldn't arrive for another ten years—a full-length Japanese raccoon polo coat that enveloped my five-foot-one frame and made me look like a short yeti—she was certain that I loved them as much as she did.

Just like Veruschka, she said when I tried the coat on in Ben's showroom. *Happy birthday, my darling.*

Her dream had come true: My mother had left the suburbs, moved back into the city, and, in her forties, was a model again. And now her daughter, whom she had always wondered about when it came to fashion, *to life itself,* was wearing a fur coat just like hers.

Twins, like twins, she said. *Wear it slouchy, just like Veruschka.*

I wore it; I hated it. When it got spray-painted outside Mr. Chow's one night in 1988 by an antifur protester, I was secretly delighted.

I ask her, on this morning, her caregiver in the other room, old sacks of makeup piled up around her like pirate's booty, why. *Why.*

A moment of tenderness and peace; we're both listening.

"Because," my mother says, "Papa told me."

She shakes her head. She flings away the magazine in disgust.

"What, Mom?"

"Papa says that I'm his homely little girl."

26

I DO NOT REMEMBER WHERE MY MOTHER WAS ON THE DAY HER father died. I do not remember seeing her when my father, who was sitting cross-legged on the living room floor in our apartment in Forest Hills on a Saturday morning in 1967, pulled me into his lap and told me that my grandfather was gone, and that wherever he was, he had loved me. I do not remember where she was when I wept at the fact of her father's death, because even at four, I understood what it meant: that I would never see him again, that life had a final and specific moment, an end point. A person could suddenly leave, and the world would change; the cast of the sky would look different. I did not see my mother that morning, and I did not call for her.

———

My grandfather, who had inherited real estate from his late mother all over Williamsburg, insisted, in his late seventies and quaking with Parkinson's, on collecting the rent on the five buildings himself. He was an old man, older than his years, frail, his body tortured by disease into a curve; he was followed into North Williamsburg near the piers where, as a child, he had eaten oysters on the waterfront in the shadow of Walt Whitman. He was robbed, beaten, and left for dead. In the emergency room, they examined him and X-rayed his chest to make sure that no ribs were broken. The doctors found a massive cancerous tumor in one of his lungs; he had been a smoker all his life with a five-pack-a-day habit. He loved unfiltered Camels, cheap cigars, a good pipe. He was taken to the New Jersey hospital where his nephew was a surgeon. They would not operate. He lived only a short time, and died there.

"The last time I saw him," my mother tells me, "I sat on the edge of his bed, and I fed him from a spoon, just like a baby."

Every year during the Jewish holidays, my mother lights four Yahrzeit candles: for Ben and for her parents, and an extra.

"—for those who don't have anyone left to pray for them," she says in the car, when Susan and I bring her to the house for dinner.

I set the table with good silver and a crisp white linen cloth, the way Gaga did when I was a child. Susan makes matzo balls—after almost twenty years of Jewish holidays, she has become an expert; they are perfect and round and light as a feather—and together we feed my mother: soup, brisket, Gaga's noodle pudding, apple cake, tea. A round challah that signifies the continuing cycle of time and the passage of years. Foods that promise a sweet new year.

"I'm not hungry," my mother says.

She cleans her plate.

A month later, at the very end of the gardening season, she returns. She has been feeling well. She wants to see us, she says, and to see the dog; it is a week before we leave for Maine. My mother stands in the vegetable garden with Susan, who will set up the lightweight hose for her. In full makeup and with her cane leaning against the side of the house, she will water the boxes, overgrown with late-season kale and winter squash and bolting lettuce. She will water the gravel and water the splintering picket fence. She will wave furiously, like a child, and tell us about the victory garden she grew in Brooklyn during the war, in the spit of urban grass between her apartment building and the next one. In the evening, we will sit her on the porch in an Adirondack chair with a glass of white wine; the neighbors will come over to say hello. We feed her, and we take her back home to the city the next day.

· · ·

"I WOULD LIKE TO LIVE to one hundred and three," my mother tells me over brunch. She takes a sip of wine.

"One hundred and three," I repeat, pushing eggs around on my plate.

We have walked together from her apartment to the bistro down the street. She is dressed in narrow dark jeans, a tight

spangled Sonia Rykiel sweater from the eighties that she un-
earthed from the living room closet, the white Air Jordans that
Susan and I bought for her when she was finally out of the
cam boots, and a long raw silk cardigan the color of straw that
comes to her knees. She is carrying her favorite blue tote,
which is filled with sheet music, compact discs, Xeroxes of her
reviews, her makeup bag. She wears thin gold hoop earrings
that graze her shoulders, and a horn link necklace that Susan
and I bought her from an artist in northern Maine. There is a
ring on every finger: the coiled snake I brought from Greece
years ago; an ivory Buddha she found in a Tibetan antiques
store on Bleecker Street an hour before Susan and I were married at Buvette, around the corner; Gaga's white-gold wedding
band.

She seems shorter now since the accident, and she clings
hard to me as we cross West End Avenue. She twirls her cane
like it's a walking stick and she's Fred Astaire.

"You need to use it, Ma," I say. *"Please—"*

"It's just for show," she says. "I don't need it."

She tucks it under her arm.

A breath; the space between stimulus and reaction. I can
stand right here in the middle of the street and plead with her,
the way I once did in my twenties after dinner with Ben and his
friends when I was drunk and taunting the traffic, wanting all
of it—the anger, the rage, the yearning—to stop. I can remind
her what the last two years have been: the surgeries, the pain,
the rehabilitation, the caregiver she hated, the wheelchair, the
money that is gone.

I let it go.

We pass a playground thronged with young children. My

mother stops to watch. The little ones climb monkey bars, play tag, play catch. They shout and squeal; a little boy, maybe three years old, straight brown hair hanging long to his shoulders, runs to the bench where a young woman—his mother? his au pair?—sits reading the newspaper. He is thrilled with something he can barely explain to her. He can't contain himself. His joy, pure and complete, bubbles like a volcano. She listens to him with rapt attention, her eyes wide with interest. He beams; there is something, a secret, that he is proud of. She lifts him into her lap, hugs him, puts him back down, and he runs off into the fray.

"He's *beautiful,*" my mother says, pointing at him. She smiles at the woman and waves.

She leans her cane against the chain-link fence that separates the street from the schoolyard. She pulls off her gloves—the forest-green ones I bought for her years ago on my first trip to Florence—and stuffs them into her tote bag. She looks into the schoolyard, her eyes glistening.

"What's wrong, Ma—"

She grabs my hand and holds it in her coat pocket, like a child's. She squeezes it hard, picks up her cane, and turns east, toward the bistro.

"Let's keep going," she says.

Afterword

THIS IS NOT THE BOOK I ENVISIONED WHEN I FIRST SAT DOWN
to write it.

On a snowy night in 2016, a few weeks after the cata-
strophic accident that would require my constant presence in
my mother's life—a fate that I had struggled for years to
escape—my editor came for dinner.

"How will this fall change your story?" she asked. "Because," she said, "it *will* change your story."

It was early in the process. My first drafts focused on the
past: our past, my past, and the moment when my mother
ceased to see me as a child, and instead recognized me as an
independent woman—a stranger so utterly different from herself that the very *fact* of me was a betrayal. Initially, my own
anger, frustration, and blindness at being her lifelong emotional

caregiver and effective spouse were primary threads, along with the trifecta that inevitably came with them: depression, addiction, and darkest humor. The cords were visceral, ancient, and osmotic: My grandmother's rage begat my mother's, and my mother's begat mine, and tugged our story along like a wagon behind a child. In the earliest versions of *Motherland*, vulnerability was elusive.

Writing this book while my mother was—and is—still alive also meant navigating the practical and moral complexities of constructing a story from the inside while it was still unfolding. Authors who write about their relationship with a parent (Frank Conroy, Kathryn Harrison, Tobias Wolff, Mary Gordon, and Sue Miller, among others) usually do so after that parent is gone. They approach their subject with the perspective and safety of time, and the tempering of grief. I had chosen not to wait. I wanted to excavate meaning from our story, to understand how a mother and daughter so tightly knitted to each other can simultaneously manage to survive half a century of enmity and still find love—the human constitution is a powerful thing. In *Motherland*, I wanted to know not who we were, but who we *are*, together; I *had* to know. I yearned for clarity and context. I would not write from a place of conjecture or speculation; I would write from a place of observation and self-scrutiny. More than anything, I wanted to heal our very thorny and fraught relationship while there was still time—assuming it was possible.

———————

My mother's accident ignited my father's prophecy, revealed in the first part of the story: *I would have to take care of her. Her care would be my job.* In the months following her fall and surgery, my exposure to her increased; it had to. We spent our days fending off ancient engraved furies and instead told each other stories. We fought; we raged. And then I listened, and she listened. *Motherland* morphed from a memoir written only from a place of codependence and my ferocious devotion to a mother carapaced by beauty against the ravages of time like a beetle in amber, to one written from the point of view of the present, with its attendant issues of reality: caregiving, dwindling resources, Talmudic expectation, age. By the time *Motherland* was completed, our roles had reversed. She became the child I never had, in whose face was drawn the purest manifestations of humanity unvarnished: fear of the unknown, and love. And *Motherland* went from being my story of survival to one of mutual vulnerability and a profound if complicated affection that belongs to us both.

Acknowledgments

In the two years during which I was actively writing this book, the narrative took me to places I could never have expected or predicted. At root, this is a love story, and without my mother, there would *be* no story, no parallel tale of survival, no beauty, no profoundly complicated affection worth struggling to unravel and heal. It has not always been easy, but it has always *been*, and I am forever grateful to my mother for her generosity of spirit, unflagging energy, style, humor and bravery, resilience, and fierce affection. But *Motherland*'s creation has taken far longer than two years: for as long as I can remember, I have been writing about the complicated character that is not only my relationship with my mother but most if not all mother-daughter relationships in their furious primacy. To be able to untangle it in real time, as it is still going on, still unfolding, has been a priceless if exigent gift, built on the promise and hope of understanding. I would not have been able to accomplish this work had it not been for the steadfast guidance and wisdom of so many who supported and empowered me along the way, both in word and action.

To my dear friend, the late author, chef, and community leader Kurt Michael Friese, who passed away suddenly in the last hours of my work on this book, and who held me, intractably, to the highest standards of compassion and kindness, I will be forever grateful. To those whose work bolsters and inspires me: Marie Howe, Kate Christensen, Claire Messud, Patricia Hampl, Terry Tempest Williams, Mark Doty, Jacki Lyden, Annie Dillard, Nigella Lawson, Diana Henry, Heidi Swanson, Anne Lamott, Molly O'Neill, Martha Frankel, Andrea Gentl and Martin Hyers. To Krista Tippett, Parker Palmer, Tobeya Ibatayo, and all those I met at the On Being Gathering, and who make the promise of resilience and reconciliation both a necessity and reality; thank you. To Joe Yonan at *The Washington Post*, who gave me a column and the opportunity to begin telling this story in *Feeding My Mother*, thank you. Warmest thanks to my earliest readers, who offered invaluable feedback: Dani Shapiro, Katie Devine, Margaret Reid Boyer, Licia Morelli. Grateful thanks to Vermont Studio Center, where I began work on *Motherland*. To the Schwartzes, the Londons, the Fertigs, the Wulfsons, the Jaegers, the Puchkoffs, the Fiebers, the Turners, the Hopkins, Jean-Marie Cannon, Vanessa Feinman, the Murphys, the Latowickis, the Other Turners, the Pennarollas, the Watsons, the Brigantis, grateful thanks. To the vast team that has helped care for my mother and done so with breathtaking grace and patience, thank you. To Dan Ravelli, who kept my house from falling down around me while I was writing. Thanks to Jeff and Lynn Sternstein, Stevie and Porter Boggess, Louise and Mark Carpentier, Michael Maren, Jane Green, Cha Tekeli, Lisa Feuer and Alyssa Awe, The Frieses, Maki Hoashi, RF Jurjevics, Laura Zimmerman and Joey Johns, Liz Queler and Seth Farber, David and Rachel Slavin, Jacqueline Church and Caleb Ho, Deborah Madison and Patrick McFarlin, The Glin Group, Imen McDonnell, Cliodhna Prendergast, Catherine and Sootie Fitzgerald, Rebecca Gleason, and Cynthia Barrett. To Tara Barker and my friends in Maine, which continues to be my safe place and where I drop my anchor: thank you.

To my dream editor, Pamela Cannon; her assistants Hanna Gibeau and Erin Kane; the extraordinary team at Ballantine Books—Ted Allen, Benjamin Dreyer, Marietta Anastassatos, Taylor Noel, Melanie DeNardo, Kara Welsh, Matthew Martin; copy editor Emily DeHuff; and to my brilliant, tough, wise agent Heather Jackson: thank you.

To my love, Susan Turner, who lights my way and is my home.

E.M.A.

January 2019

About the Author

ELISSA ALTMAN is the author of *Poor Man's Feast: A Love Story of Comfort, Desire, and the Art of Simple Cooking* and the James Beard Award–winning blog of the same name and *Treyf: My Life as an Unorthodox Outlaw*. Her work has appeared in *O: The Oprah Magazine, The Wall Street Journal, The Guardian, The New York Times, Tin House, The Rumpus, Dame Magazine, LitHub, Saveur,* and *The Washington Post,* where her column, "Feeding My Mother," ran for a year. Her work has been anthologized in *Best Food Writing* six times. A finalist for the Frank McCourt Memoir Prize, Altman has taught the craft of memoir at The Fine Arts Work Center in Provincetown, The Loft Literary Center, 1440 Multiversity, and Ireland's Literature and Larder Program, and has appeared live onstage at TEDx and The Public, on Heritage Radio, and widely on NPR. She lives in Connecticut with her family.

elissaaltman.com
Facebook.com/elissa.altman
Twitter: @ElissaAltman
Instagram: @elissa_altman

About the Type

This book was set in Fairfield, the first typeface from the hand of the distinguished American artist and engraver Rudolph Ruzicka (1883–1978). Ruzicka was born in Bohemia (in the present-day Czech Republic) and came to America in 1894. He set up his own shop, devoted to wood engraving and printing, in New York in 1913 after a varied career working as a wood engraver, in photoengraving and banknote printing plants, and as an art director and freelance artist. He designed and illustrated many books, and was the creator of a considerable list of individual prints—wood engravings, line engravings on copper, and aquatints.